Save Thousands
Buying Your Home

Save Thousands Buying Your Home

A step-by-step guide to reducing the price of a house and the cost of your mortgage

2nd edition

MAXWELL HODSON

howtobooks

Published by How To Books Ltd,
3 Newtec Place, Magdalen Road,
Oxford, OX4 1RE, United Kingdom.
Tel: (01865) 793806. Fax: (01865) 248780.
email: info@howtobooks.co.uk
www.howtobooks.co.uk

First edition 2001
Second edition 2003

British Library Cataloguing in Publication Data.
A catalogue record for this book is available from the British Library.

Cartoons by Mike Flanagan
Cover design by Baseline Arts Ltd, Oxford

Produced for How To Books by Deer Park Productions
Typeset by Anneset, Weston-super-Mare, Somerset
Printed and bound by Cromwell Press, Trowbridge, Wiltshire

Note: The material contained in this book is set out in good faith for
general guidance and no liability can be accepted for loss or expense
incurred as a result of relying in particular circumstances on statements
made in this book. Laws and regulations may be complex and liable to
change, and readers should check the current position with the relevant
authorities before making personal arrangements.

Contents

List of Illustrations

Preface

I have used my previous experience as a financial adviser and spent four years researching buying homes to write this book. I felt that there wasn't a book on the market that helped people to save the maximum amount of money on the cost of their home. There are many good books on buying your home, saving money on mortgages or building your home. There didn't seem to be one that put everything together to help you save money on your home. Whilst writing this book I have used the information in it to save myself over £2,000 a year which could mean a saving of over £40,000 over 20 years. You could do the same or better.

I have made many mistakes buying property and arranging mortgages but I have learnt from these mistakes. If I had learnt what is in this book earlier I would have saved tens of thousands of pounds.

The first half of the book deals with purchasing your home as cheaply as possible. In Chapter 1 on auctions you can find out how a £20,000 flat was bought for £140. In Chapter 2 on building your own home you can find out how a £275,000 house was built for £175,000. In Chapter 3 on negotiating you can find out how to reduce the cost of everything from solicitors' fees to removal costs. In Chapter 4 on buying on limited means you can find out how to pay half the cost of a property.

The second part of the book deals with getting good financial advice and paying as little as possible on your mortgage. Chapter 5 describes how to obtain good financial advice. Chapter 6 explains mortgages and shows you the advantages and disadvantages of repayment and interest only mortgages. Chapter 7 on reducing the cost of your mortgage shows you how you could save £22,384 on a 25-year £70,000 mortgage at 5.2%. Chapter 8 on reducing your ongoing home costs will show you how you can get a 30% return on your money. Chapter 9 on remortgages will show you how I saved £140 a month on the cost of my mortgage.

If you only read one chapter in this book then read Chapter 10. This chapter shows you how much you can save by applying all the principles in this book together. You will be shown how someone can buy their home for half price. You will also find out how I saved £2,000 a year. If you do nothing with this book you will save nothing. If you apply the information in this book you can save tens of thousands of pounds. I wish you all the best and hope you save a lot of money on the cost of your home.

Many people have helped me in writing this book. I would particularly like to thank for their invaluable assistance: Paul Padmore, Rob Hodson, Darren Hodson, Martin Allport at the Yorkshire Bank, Tony Wood and Scott Mowbray at Virgin. I would also like to thank everyone at How To Books for their guidance and for giving me the chance to publish this book. Finally I would like to thank my wife Bridget who believed in me and helped me so much. I would like to dedicate this book to Bridget, Katie, Emily, my parents and brothers. I love you all so much.

Maxwell Hodson

1

Buying at Auction

ADVANTAGES AND DISADVANTAGES OF BUYING AT AUCTION

Buying a property at auction can save you a great deal of money. The main advantages of buying at auction are:

- You can get a potential bargain.

- Once the hammer has gone down the property is legally yours and you can't be gazumped.

- Buying a property through an auction can take as little as three weeks.

The disadvantages of an auction are:

- An auction can be very stressful.

- You are advised to arrange a survey before the auction and if you don't buy the property you will lose the money you paid for the survey.

- A survey is compulsory if you are purchasing via a mortgage.

- You can overbid and pay too much for the property.

Property auctions are becoming more and more popular with the general public, and they do offer a way of getting a bargain home, provided you take time and care. More private vendors are now putting their houses up for sale by auction because they want a quick, clean sale. There are also problem properties and repossessions which can be particularly cheap – however, you need to take care with these.

UNDERSTANDING THE AUCTION PROCESS

The first step to take if you are considering buying a property at auction is to decide on the area in which you want to buy your house and contact an auctioneer who deals with properties in that area.

It is important that you go to an auction first to make sure that you are comfortable with the auction process. Auctions can be stressful but thrilling. You must go and see what an auction is like before you seriously decide to buy through one.

The auction process is different from a normal house sale through an estate agent. In an auction the property is 'knocked down' to the bidder: the bidder exchanges contracts with the auctioneer there and then and cannot back out of the purchase later. The buyer is legally bound to it, even if he leaves the saleroom without signing anything.

You therefore have to arrange all the surveys and finance before the auction. This is often a rush to arrange if the purchase is intended to be in connection with a mortgage. In this case both the survey fee and the legal costs (for the work done to date) are at risk, if the sale does not proceed. If the survey is not arranged in time or the lender has not agreed to accept the mortgage by the time of the auction, the lender may not accept the mortgage for underwriting reasons. The lender may need their own survey to be carried out to approve a mortgage, therefore do not carry out your own survey until you have checked with the lender.

If you require a mortgage to buy a property it is often a good idea to obtain a mortgage promise from the lender before you go house hunting. In this case all the preliminary work is then completed by the lender, hence only a survey would be required to provide an offer.

It is essential to be prepared even before you get to the auction. You need to contact the auctioneers who deal with your area and ask them for a brochure – Winkworths, for example, will send you a full-colour catalogue three weeks before their monthly auction. The catalogue will contain information about 50 to 100 properties and details on how to view them.

GETTING THE PRICE RIGHT

Making an offer before auction

The publicity for a property to be sold at auction may contain the proviso, 'unless previously sold'. In this case the seller's agent is open to offers and is prepared to negotiate a sale in the normal way, before and instead of an auction. The seller will, however, probably still expect to sell on an auction contract, and you may therefore only have a few days to do the surveys and raise the funds. It is always worth asking the agents if you can make an offer for a property before auction. The outcome of an auction is uncertain in that the seller doesn't know what price he will get for a property; therefore if you make an offer before the auction you may save yourself a lot of money and stress.

Reaching the reserve price

Some properties which are being sold by executors or creditors will have to go to auction for legal reasons connected with proving that the proper price has been obtained. If the property is one of these, you will see a phrase such as 'sold by order of the executors or trustees'. In this case do not make an offer prior to the auction because this may affect the reserve price.

The **reserve price** is the price that must be reached for the property to be sold. You need to check whether one of the seller's conditions is selling 'subject to a reserve price'. The reserve price will not usually be disclosed, although the selling agent may give you a guideline figure. During the bidding, the agent may use a phrase such as 'I am going to sell this property' as an indication that the reserve price has been reached. If the bidding does not reach the reserve price the auctioneer will withdraw the property. If you are among the last bidders when the property is withdrawn, tell the agent afterwards at what figure you were prepared to buy – the seller may accept your offer.

Avoid overbidding

One particularly important point is that you must be careful not to overbid. If you bid more than your mortgage lender is willing to lend, you will have to find the difference. It can often be a good idea to ask someone else to bid for you, such as a solicitor, and give them a maximum figure that you can bid up to.

SUMMARY OF THE AUCTION PROCESS

1. It is very important to study the agent's brochure extremely carefully, reading all the small print. There may be conditions or disclaimers which would make the property unsuitable. Look for mention of any planning restrictions or refusals in case you might wish to make any alterations or improvements.

2. View the house in the normal way and make sure it is what you want. Remember, you can't back out after the auction.

3. Send the brochure to your solicitor or licensed conveyancer as early as possible for them to carry out the usual enquiries and searches and check title before the day of the auction. Arrange for a survey and valuation to be done and get the results before the auction.

4. Fix your price limit and have the arrangements for the necessary finance ready in place before the auction.

5. If you are successful you will have to pay 10% of your bid to the auctioneer straight away. The Memorandum of Agreement is countersigned by the seller's agent as confirmation of the sale and acknowledgement of receipt of the 10% deposit. The rest of the sale follows as a normal house sale.

SALE BY TENDER

An alternative to an auction is a sale by tender. When a property is being sold by tender you are invited to put your offer, together with a 10% deposit, in a sealed envelope and send it to the agent by a specified date. Then the envelopes are opened and the highest offer purchases the property. A 'Form of Tender' is included in the sale particulars. It is important to check whether the terms of the tender include a contract, in which case you may be bound to purchase. In other cases you may still be able to back out after your tender has been accepted.

LIST OF AUCTIONEERS

Allsop & Co.	020 7437 6977	www.allsopp.co.uk
Athawes Son & Co.	020 8992 0056	
Hambro Countrywide	01245 344 133	
Halifax Property Services	01482 228 400	www.halifax.co.uk
Jones and Chapman	01253 612 000	www.wheretolive.co.uk
Roy Pugh	01772 883 399	www.pugh-company.co.uk
Winkworths	020 8649 7255	www.eigroup.co.uk

- An independent company called Faxwise will send you catalogues and details of all property auctions for three months at a cost of £100. For details Tel: 020 7720 5000.

- A company called P.D.S is a property brokerage dealing exclusively with repossessed properties, land and properties in need of refurbishment and renovation. For details Tel: 01494 444096.

- The *Estate Gazette* contains details of auction houses, current prices and auctions. It is worth ordering a copy from your newsagents.

WHAT CAN BE ACHIEVED AT AUCTION?

Here are some examples to show you what kinds of bargains can be achieved at auction. You may be amazed!

- A £20,000 flat bought for £140!

  BBC *Watchdog* found the cheapest flat in Britain. It was a one-bedroom flat in Salford, Greater Manchester, with double-glazing, central heating, a fitted kitchen, and carpets. The flat had also got the use of the building's gym and sauna. It was bought at auction for £140!

- A £49,000 flat bought for £13,500!

  A TV documentary called *A Little Xtra Help* on BBC 2 showed the example of a flat in a desirable residence that was originally purchased for £49,000. An offer of £40,000 was made for the property but the building society still decided to reposssess it. The flat was sold at auction for £13,500.

- A £35,000 property bought for £95!

  A man bought a property at auction for £1,900; since he got a 95% mortgage to buy it he only actually paid £95 for the property. (5% of £1,900 = £95). He renovated the property and six months later sold it for £35,000.

Here are a few more examples:

- 24 acres of woodland for £1,500
- an up-and-running public house for £10,500
- a central London apartment for £18,000
- a holiday home in Cornwall for £15,000
- a first-floor apartment for £4,200

These are just a few examples of the bargains which can be obtained at auctions. *You* can buy some of these bargains – but you need to do your homework.

CHECKLIST

- Arrange to go to an auction and make sure that you are comfortable with the auction process.
- Contact the auctioneers who deal in property in your chosen area and get them to send you a brochure.

- View the house(s) you are interested in.

- Arrange a survey on the house.

- Send the brochure and details to your solicitor/conveyancer for them to check the title, arrange searches and make the usual enquiries.

- Arrange the finance.

- Fix your price limit.

- If successful pay the 10% deposit to the auctioneer and obtain a Memorandum of Agreement.

- Let your solicitor or conveyancer complete the sale.

2

Building Your Own Home

By building your own home you can save on average a third of the price that the completed house would cost you. You can even save up to half the cost of the house if you are prepared to plan carefully and do more of the work yourself.

> Paul bought a piece of land for £85,000. He spent the next six months building a house using builders, plumbers and electricians. He found the workmen to be particularly frustrating because some of them failed to turn up to do the required work. The building cost £90,000. The total cost came to £175,000. The property was, however, finally valued at £275,000, a profit of £100,000.

ADVANTAGES AND DISADVANTAGES OF BUILDING YOUR OWN HOME

Some of the **advantages** of building your own house are:

- You can save 30% to 50% of the house price.

- You will be designing your own house and getting the house you want, not what a builder has designed.

- You can specify the requirements in the house; for example, 8 inches of roof insulation, double glazing, etc.

- You have the independence and adventure of building your own home.

- You have the satisfaction of tackling and completing a large project.

Some of the **disadvantages** are:

- Building your own home can be stressful.

- If you decide to build it yourself you may have to devote long hours to the work.

- Accommodation for you and your family while you are building can be difficult to arrange.

- The work is often dirty and messy.

- There is a risk when building your own property that there may be problems with the building (e.g. structural problems and any number of other things).

KNOWING HOW TO BUILD YOUR OWN PROPERTY

We will now look at the process of building your own property to give you an idea of what is entailed. This will not be a detailed guide since there are many good books devoted to the subject, some of which are listed at the end of this chapter.

Finding the land or property

The first stage is to look for a suitable piece of land or run-down property. You may decide that you want to build your house from scratch, or you can convert a barn or other property to suit yourself. You need to approach landowners and farmers in the area for a suitable plot. It is preferable to obtain a piece of land that has got planning consent. Also try and look for land that has services (electricity, sewerage and roads) nearby because it can be extremely expensive to lay long lengths of pipework. Estate agents may have some plots available, and there are also a number of companies which have plots of land for sale. Local authorities can also have plots of land for sale that often have planning consent.

Outline planning consent

The next stage is to make sure the land or property has outline planning consent. Outline consent means that, in the view of the local authority planning committee, the land in question may accommodate a building, the exact nature of which will be decided later. It is possible to negotiate a position on a field whereby you apply for, and receive, outline planning consent before you purchase the field. The land, not the applicant, bears the consent (or lack of consent). You can buy land or property without planning consent, but it is risky. You could end up with a plot you can't build on. The local authority will require a rough drawing of the type of property you intend to build. There will also be the costs imposed by the local authority for the planning application.

Solicitor's checks

You need to get a solicitor to check the title of the land you want to buy. It is essential that there are no restrictive covenants or easements which may affect your building in some way. The solicitor will carry out a variety of searches which will interrogate the local authority about their future plans for the area and the plot in question.

Architect's plans

Once you have decided that you want to buy the land you need to approach a suitably qualified architect or draughtsman. Qualified architects have the letters RIBA after their name which denotes their membership of the Royal Institute of British Architects. Professional architects are familiar with dealing in with planning applications and may well be known by officials of the local authority. You need to arrange a sketch scheme based on your ideas and drawings. The architect will draw it and advise you about obtaining planning permission. When you are happy with the plans, instruct the architect to apply for planning permission.

Raising finance

You may need to arrange finance for the project. In general you will need to purchase the land for the project yourself, but the rest of the project can be aided by mortgage lenders. Before you approach a lender you will need a good idea of the cost of the whole job. To obtain the finance you can be helped by an independent financial adviser or a mortgage broker (see Chapter 5).

Starting to build

Once planning permission has been granted, the architect should be instructed to prepare working drawings for submission to the Building Control Department of the local authority. A **building inspector** will then visit the site at your request to inspect specified stages of the work. Building inspectors cannot be made liable for commercial loss, and this should be borne in mind when seeking their advice. You will be given a set of postcards which will summon the inspector when each phase is complete and ready for inspection. It is your duty to give the inspector adequate warning that a stage is about to reach completion. On no account must you progress to the next stage before he has visited the site.

- **Subcontractors** are able to work out prices for their various tasks from the architect's working drawings. Always get three separate subcontractors to quote for each job.

- Make sure you have **self build insurance**.

- Some builders will complete the whole process for you instead of using an architect and they can be much cheaper.

- Builders must have an **NHBC certificate** otherwise lenders may not lend money for the house. If you don't get an NHBC certificate you may not be able to sell your property within ten years of building it.

- Builders and architects will provide estimates for you and sometimes they can provide fixed quotes.

- It can often be the least frustrating if you hand over the project to one builder rather than trying to deal with a number of people.

Completing the building

Providing you follow the steps above, you should be able to finish the project. There may be a number of finishing jobs which will take longer to complete, such as the garden. The steps shown above for building your house are an outline. There are several good books on the subject which are listed later: these books are much more detailed and will give you very good advice on the whole process.

Mr and Mrs Jessop decided to have a timber frame house built to their specification. They had to spend a long time looking for a suitable piece of land, but eventually they found it. They bought an old mobile home to live in while they built the house. The house took ten months to build: they ran into cash flow problems along the way, having used up most of their money buying the land, and had to arrange staged payments from a mortgage company. The mortgage company made payments on completion of specified stages of the house. By the time the timber frame was up, they owed £15,000 to the builder and were desperate to get the roof on so that the next staged payment could be made. The house was, however, eventually finished. The land had cost them £47,000 and the building £94,500: the total cost therefore was £141,500. The final valuation of the house was £215,000.

SOME TIPS FOR SELF-BUILDERS

- When you plan a project, make sure that you have enough cash flow to keep things going.

- Keep a running total of your build costs and stick to your budget, otherwise expenditure can get completely out of hand, or let an architect or builder handle the project.

- Establish a rapport with your local builder's merchant and ask all your suppliers to help you when calculating materials required, in order to avoid under- or over-ordering.

- Enquire about setting up an account with suppliers to obtain cheaper building supplies.

- Deal with a well-established company, or at least one which you know will provide you with the support you need. It is comforting to know that someone is always available on the end of a telephone.

- Consider living on site – it can be a deterrent to petty thieves. Building sites are a prime target and with expensive tools and materials around, it is better to keep a close eye on them.

- Be prepared for lots of hard work and very little leisure time (unless you pay someone else to build it).

- Try to think of absolutely everything in your budget: for example, a planner's insistence on making a chimney larger will have a financial impact.

- Ensure that all contractors sign a contract so that bad workmanship can be rectified.

MORTGAGES FOR SELF-BUILDERS

There are two types of mortgages for self-builders. These are advance stage payment mortgages and arrear stage payment mortgages. The advance stage mortgages will release funds in advance of each building stage. This gives the self-builder positive cash flow which means that more self-builders can remain in their current house while their new house is being built. The arrear stage mortgages only allow funds to be released after certain specified stages have been completed. There are a number of lenders that will provide self-build mortgages: Figure 1 gives some examples. The best advice is to contact a good financial adviser (IFA) who can search through the many lenders to find the best mortgage for you.

Lender and telephone no.	Type of Mortgage	Stage required for first payment	LTV on Land	Final LTV and building
Britannia BS 0870 872 0908	Accelerator	Funds paid in advance	95%	95%
Lloyds TSB 0870 872 0908	Accelerator	Funds paid in advance	95%	95%
Skipton BS 0870 872 0908	Accelerator	Funds paid in advance	95%	95%
Cambridge BS 01223 727 727	Arrear	First floor joists	no	80%
Ecology BS 0845 6745566	Arrear	flexible	85%	85%
Ipswich BS 01473 211021	Arrear	foundations	80%	95%
Kent Reliance 01634 848944	Arrear	Brickwork and partitions	25%	75%
Northern Rock 0845 6050500	Arrear	Wind and water tight	no	95%
Shepshed BS 01509 822000	Arrear	Flexible	66%	95%
Stroud and Swindon Swindon 0800 616112	Arrear	First floor joists	75%	65%

Fig. 1. Self-build mortgages: examples of lenders
(LTV = Loan to Value).

The following lenders will also consider self-build mortgages on an individual basis:

- Clydesdale Bank
- Bristol West
- Cheshire Building Society
- First Direct
- First Trust Bank
- Homesdale Building Society.

FURTHER INFORMATION SOURCES

Build It – this magazine covers all aspects of designing and building your own home. Available from newsagents.

Building your Own Home (300 pages) – deals with every aspect of building your own home. Tel: 01909 591652.

The Complete and Essential Guide to Building your Own Home by Rosalind Renshaw (200 pages). Advice and information on all aspects of building a house. Tel: 020 7865 9042.

The Housebuilders Bible – covers all aspects of building a house, written by a self-builder. Tel: 01223 290230.

Insurance for self-building

DMS Services Ltd. Tel: 01909 591652.

Holbrook Insurance Brokers. Tel: 01483 505932.

Plots of land

Build It magazine often lists plots of land for sale.

Landbank Services Ltd. Tel: 0118 962 6022.

Natural Plotfinder Database. Tel: 0906 557 5400.

Websites

Home Builder (self-build information)   www.gold.net

Self Build and Design magazine   www.selfbuildanddesign.com

Homebuilding magazine   www.homebuilding.co.uk

CHECKLIST

- Buy one of the recommended books.
- Buy some copies of *Build It* magazine.
- Find a piece of land, preferably with planning consent.
- Obtain outline planning consent.
- Arrange for your solicitors to carry out the necessary checks.

- Purchase the land and look into arranging the finance for the property.

- Arrange for the architect to do the drawings for the house and apply for planning permission.

- Arrange the finance.

- Start the building process.

- Make sure you get three quotes for everything you need.

- Make sure you plan your cash flow and ensure it is enough for the project.

- Keep a running total of the costs and stick to your budget or let a builder or architect do it for you.

- Try to deal with well-established companies.

- Consider living on the site.

- Spend time on your budget and try to plan everything.

3

Negotiating to Reduce Your Home Costs

This chapter is about negotiating how much you pay for your house and the costs involved in purchasing it. To help reduce the cost of buying your house you can negotiate on all of the following:

- solicitors' costs

- Stamp Duty

- Mortgage Indemnity Guarantee Premium

- valuation fees

- mortgage arrangement fees

- estate agents' fees

- house removal fees

- mortgage rate

- house price

- extras that can be included with the house

- costs of building your home

- financial advisers' costs.

You can negotiate a better price on many more costs than people realise. First we will look at the negotiating process, then we will look at each of these costs and examine how you can negotiate a cheaper price.

UNDERSTANDING THE PRINCIPLES OF NEGOTIATING

Most people don't like negotiating, but it is much easier than you think. You can save yourself thousands of pounds if you negotiate. All negotiating is, initially, is asking. The reality is that negotiating is easy – children are great at it! They negotiate to stay out late, get more pocket money and any number of other things. Their secret is that they know exactly what they want and are determined to push for it. You need to concentrate on a number of points when negotiating:

- Negotiating is simply asking.

- If you don't ask you don't get.

- Spend time doing some research to improve your chances of success.

- Get quotes and prices from a number of sources to help you to negotiate a reduced price.

- Consider what the seller wants; for example, he may reduce the price for a quick clean sale.

- Always remember you have the freedom to go to another competitor.

- You can often confer additional benefits to the other party; for example, when arranging a mortgage you can move your bank account to the lender.

- You can often give the other party non-financial benefits such as more self-esteem.

We will now look at each of the areas where negotiation is possible.

SOLICITORS' COSTS

You need to get three quotes from solicitors, then contact your preferred solicitors and see if they will reduce their prices compared to the cheapest quote. Their costs are not set in stone and they can be negotiated. You can also get a quote from a fixed-fee solicitor to help you negotiate.

- Fixed price conveyancing: contact Central Legal and Conveyancing. Tel: 0808 1446343.

- Check the *Yellow Pages* under Solicitors or Conveyancers.

- You can also ask for recommendations from friends. Get two or three quotes.

It is very important to get quotes from solicitors first. One seventy-five-year-old lady was charged £5,500 by her solicitor for selling her flat. The sale was straightforward because she sold it to the neighbour downstairs but the solicitor had negotiated the sale incurring the extra costs. The lady should have got a quote first.

STAMP DUTY

You can't directly negotiate to reduce your Stamp Duty, but you can reduce it by negotiating for a reduction in the price of the house. The Stamp Duty on house purchases is currently as shown in Figure 2.

House price	£0 – £59,999	£60,000 – £249,999	£250,000 – £499,999	£500,000 +
Stamp Duty	0	1%	2.5%	3.5%

Fig. 2. Stamp Duty rates.

If, for example, a property cost £61,000 you would have to pay £61,000 plus £610 Stamp Duty. If you could negotiate the price down to £59,995, you would pay £59,995 and no Stamp Duty. Therefore, you would save yourself £1,615 by negotiating a price that was £1,005 cheaper.

If the vendor of the house will not reduce the price it may be possible to negotiate for the price to be shown as lower, but then to pay extra for fittings such as carpets and curtains. For example, if the house cost £61,000 you could negotiate to pay £59,995 for the house and £1,005 separately for the carpets and curtains. This would save you £610 in Stamp Duty. You have to be careful with this tactic because the government does not want to lose Stamp Duty: it is only possible if the price is close to the bottom of one of the Stamp Duty bands.

MORTGAGE INDEMNITY GUARANTEE PREMIUM (MIG)

Most people will not negotiate with banks or building societies after a mortgage offer has been made. You must remember that banks and building societies are now in a competitive mortgage market and are more willing to negotiate on the pricing of their mortgage products. You need to ask if they will reduce or get rid of the Mortgage Indemnity Premium (MIG) – remember that there are other lenders, such as the Cheltenham & Gloucester and Direct Line, who don't charge MIG. Go armed with this information to the bank or building society, and always remember that you can take your business and personal account elsewhere.

The MIG covers mortgage lenders against the added risk involved in advancing higher loans, that is mortgages of more than approximately 75% of the property's value. The insurance covers any losses incurred by the lender if the borrower defaults and the property has to be repossessed and sold. The MIG is of no benefit to you the borrower. It only benefits the lender. Under the process of subrogation the insurer can chase the defaulting home-owner for any amount paid out on the insurance. The insurer has the right to pursue the borrower for 12 years, so a repossession could come back to haunt you over a decade after you have surrendered your home.

MIG is normally a single one-off-payment but it can be added to the mortgage or with some lenders it can be paid off over various terms. The cheapest way if you have to pay MIG is to pay it in a single lump sum. There are two main ways of reducing the MIG you will pay:

● The larger the deposit you put down on your house the less MIG you will pay. If you pay a 25% deposit or more you will not have to pay MIG with most lenders.

● You can choose a lender that charges no MIG or has low rates.

Contact an independent financial adviser for advice.

VALUATION FEES

Valuation fees are not set in stone. There are three types of survey: a standard survey, a homebuyer's survey and a structural survey. A standard survey is the cheapest and the structural survey is the most expensive. It is always advisable to have a good survey done because it can show up potential problems. You can also use the survey to negotiate a reduced price if it shows that work needs to be done on the property. If it is an old property or in a poor state of repair, have a structural survey done.

Some lenders will insist on having their own survey done so make sure you check this before you arrange your own survey. Lenders may also insist on further surveys on damp or electrical problems if they see fit.

If possible you need to get three quotes for the valuation that you need, then you can use the cheapest quote to go back to the other valuers and see if they will match or better it.

MORTGAGE ARRANGEMENT FEES

Arrangement fees seem to be charged on fixed rate mortgages; however, there are many mortgages on which these fees are not charged. If the mortgage that appeals to you is subject to arrangement fees, look through the mortgage market to see if there are any similar mortgages without arrangement fees. If there are, you can go back to the original lender and ask them to waive the arrangement fee. Remember, you have the power of choice: tell the lenders that you are going to use it!

ESTATE AGENTS' FEES

It is important when selling your house through estate agents that you get three quotes. Estate agents' fees vary: they may charge a fixed fee, a variable fee depending on the selling price, or 'no sale – no fee'. It is important to spend time looking at which estate agent's package will suit you best. Once you have decided on the best package you can then use the quotes to try and get a cheaper quote. Additional methods you may try are prompt payment of their fees, pre-paying their fees, and letting them have the sole sale (instead of putting your house with a number of estate agents to try to get a quick sale) – all these may help you to negotiate a better price.

HOUSE REMOVAL FEES

It is important to get three quotes for house removal fees as they can vary a great deal between companies. Obtain some quotes from smaller local companies who may offer a more competitive price to get the business. The important point to note about removal fees is that you can arrange the removal yourself to save the most money. You can use this to your advantage when trying to get cheaper removal fees – tell the removal company that you will do the removal yourself unless they reduce their prices.

MORTGAGE RATE

Most people believe that you can't negotiate or change the mortgage rate once you have arranged a mortgage. A small number of people have found out to their advantage that they can negotiate better rates. Remortgaging is a very competitive business. Lenders are aware of this and they are very keen both to get new business and to hold on to existing business.

You can investigate reducing your mortgage rate if you have a variable rate and no penalty clauses for redemption of the mortgage. If you are looking for a lower variable rate, look first of all at direct lenders. Phone a number of direct lenders, and go through the mortgage process with them on the phone. Do not complete the mortgage process with them at this stage: arrange for the direct lender to send you the details in the post and check that they will provisionally offer you the mortgage.

The next stage is to go to your current lender, show them the better mortgage rate that you have been offered, and ask them to match or better that rate, otherwise you will move your mortgage. As added pressure, if you bank with your current lender you can threaten to move your bank account as well. Give your current lender some time to come back to you, but set a time limit for an answer.

If your lender doesn't offer to match or better the rate, you can look at remortgaging. Chapter 9 on remortgaging will give you an idea of the costs involved. Many current lenders will, however, be keen to keep your custom and will lower your mortgage rate. Either way, you may be able to save yourself a lot of money by getting a better mortgage rate.

Many mortgages also have redemption fees if you redeem the mortgage early. This can be costly if you are locked into a bad mortgage product; for example, a high interest rate when mortgage rates are falling. Many people have negotiated to waive these penalties. Therefore don't automatically pay these penalties if you have to move your mortgage.

HOUSE PRICE

This is an important area where you can save money by negotiating. A saving of £1,000 off the price is worth much more if you have to pay this on a mortgage. As an example, £1,000 on a 25-year repayment mortgage, at 5.75% interest without tax relief, would cost you £6.36 per month, a total of £1,908 over the 25-year period; so if you could save £1,000 off the price of the house, it would be worth £1,908 to you. It pays to negotiate the price of the house down. Here are some important questions to ask:

- **How eager is the vendor to sell?**
  You can talk to the vendor or his estate agent about his reasons for selling the house. If they won't tell you directly, you may be able to pick up clues in conversation. If the house is with more than one estate agent, this is a big clue. You can negotiate the price down by offering a quick clean sale.

- **How realistic is the price?**
  How does the price compare with other similar properties advertised? Estate agents can give you useful information on how realistic the price is. You may also have other information which will help reduce the price – for example, the valuation report may have shown that some work needs to be done. If you are making a much lower offer than is expected, offer some evidence of why you are doing so. The evidence that supports your offer may help to lower the vendor's expectations. Always remember, it is better to start with an artificially low offer and work up, instead of making the initial offer too high.

- **Who is the vendor?**
  If the vendor is a company or building society there is a fair chance that they will want to get rid of the property quickly, and therefore you should try offering them a reduced price but with a quick sale. If the

vendor is a private vendor, does he need to move quickly because of work or other commitments?

- **What is the vendor's experience?**
  Some vendors will just make life difficult for you. Remember that you can always walk away from the deal if you aren't happy. If the vendors are inexperienced, you may be able to lower their expectations by giving them examples of similar properties that have sold for less. You may also be able to use the valuation to lower their expectations – if the valuation report indicates that work needs to be done on the property, this can be used to lower the price.

EXTRAS THAT CAN BE INCLUDED WITH THE HOUSE

A lot of extras can be negotiated for with a house sale. The most common items are carpets and curtains, which you can negotiate to have included in the price. Remember, if the house costs just over £60,000 you may be able to negotiate a price just below £60,000 for the house, but arrange to pay for carpets and curtains separately to make up the price, and in this way you will avoid paying Stamp Duty.

Anything that is in the house or in the garden can be negotiated for. It is also worth checking what the vendors intend to include with the sale. There are stories of people taking all the plants out of the garden, taking all the light bulbs and light fittings and anything else that isn't bolted down. It is important therefore that while you are viewing the house you ask what the vendors intend to include in the sale. If there are things you would particularly like – for example a garden shed, the curtains or anything else – first ask the vendors if they are included in the price. If the item you would like isn't included in the price you can try and negotiate it into the price. By including a number of 'extras' in this way you can save yourself a great deal of money. Always remember that if you don't ask, you don't get.

COSTS OF BUILDING YOUR HOME

If you decide to renovate a property or build your own home, you have a great deal of scope to save money. Firstly, you can negotiate on the price of the property or land, and you can also often negotiate for extras to be included in the price. For example, one couple, who bought a run-down property, negotiated for a mobile home to be included in the price: they then lived in the mobile home while they renovated the property until it was fit to live in.

The costs of building your house or renovating it are all negotiable. It is important to get two or three quotes for all parts of the work and materials – you can then use these quotes to try to get cheaper ones. It is important to make sure that workmen or suppliers keep to their quotes. Don't rush into the work with the first supplier or builder you contact, because they may charge you much more than you should be paying.

You can of course save yourself a great deal of money if you are prepared to do a lot of the work yourself. If you are not prepared to do this, you can save money by living on the building site – this will deter petty criminals, and in addition if you oversee the work yourself it will be done to your satisfaction and probably more quickly. You will need to check with the local authority that you can live on the site.

FINANCIAL ADVISERS' COSTS

A financial adviser makes money from advising you. This can happen in two ways: either they earn commission from the policies they recommend, or they charge you a fee. It is best to choose a financial consultant who offers you both options – this gives you the flexibility to negotiate the best deal for yourself.

Certain policies can pay very large commissions, since the commission rises as the premiums increase. If you are buying a large house which needs a large savings plan to pay off the mortgage, the commission may be sizeable – commissions are quite often several hundred pounds, and they can run into thousands for big mortgages. In certain circumstances it may be better to pay a fee which is less than the commission earned: the amount of the commission should then be paid back to you or added into your policy. On the other hand, if the commission is only going to be a small amount, it would be better for you if the financial adviser worked on a commission. The flexibility to choose gives you the best option.

A mortgage broker tends to charge a percentage of the loan on completion of the mortgage – this often varies between 1% to and 2% of the loan value. By negotiating the fees with the mortgage broker you may be able to save yourself several hundred pounds. You have the choice of which mortgage broker or financial adviser you go to – make sure you remind them of this.

CHECKLIST

● Remember that negotiating is asking, and everything can be negotiated for.

- Use information to negotiate a better price.

- Use your freedom of personal choice to negotiate.

- Use time to help you negotiate.

- Spend time preparing to negotiate: it will improve your results.

- Get three quotes for everything and use these to negotiate a reduced price.

4

Buying on Limited Means

In this chapter we will look at ways of buying houses when you have limited means and cannot afford to buy a property outright or cases where it may be difficult to get a mortgage. There are a number of options available to you which we can look at:

- sharing a mortgage

- split equity deals

- buying from local authorities

- homebuy

- housing grants

- DSS mortgages

- County Court Judgements (CCJs) and arrears

- negative equity

- self-employed.

SHARING A MORTGAGE

To reduce the cost of buying a house and the monthly mortgage cost it is possible to share a mortgage. Most mortgage lenders are happy to do this. The maximum number of people allowed is usually four as a mortgage deed only has room for four names. An application for more than four is acceptable but will need more referrals. We will now look at some of the technicalities of buying a house with one or more people:

How much can you borrow?

If there are two people sharing a mortgage you can usually borrow up to three times the main income plus one times the second income, or 2.5 times the joint income. If there are more than two people it is usually three times the main income and one times each subsequent income.

For example, if there are three people with incomes of £15,000, £10,000 and £7,000, the borrowing capacity would be £15,000 × 3 = £45,000 + £10,000 + £7,000. Total £62,000.

Do you need a legal agreement?

You should set up the mortgage deeds and a legal agreement between the people who are sharing the mortgage when the house is bought. There are different types of agreements for joint home-owners.

(a) A **joint tenancy** is usually drawn up by two people in a relationship. This type of agreement gives an equal right to remain in the property even after divorce or separation. If one owner dies the other automatically gains possession of the whole property.

(b) Where friends are buying, a **tenants-in-common agreement** is more usual. Each owner has a share of the property with which they can do as they wish. If one owner dies then their share goes to their next of kin or to whoever is nominated in their will.

To avoid any misunderstanding tenants-in-common also need to draw up a **declaration of trust** which states:

● in what proportion the property is held (usually dependent on the proportion paid towards the property)

● in what shares the running costs and bills will be paid

● how you will agree on the need for maintenance and how you will sort out payment

● who else can live in the property and under what conditions

● how much notice is needed for one party to sell urgently

● the minimum length of time before the house can be sold for non-urgent reasons

● if one party wishes to sell and the other to buy, what basis will be used for calculating a fair price and for dividing the costs of selling

● how any losses in the sale will be divided.

The tenants-in-common agreement and the declaration of trust will need to be reviewed regularly. It is also a good idea to draw up some kind of agreement if you are buying with your partner. It should cover things like what happens to the property if you separate, who gets what if the property is sold, and so on.

The drawbacks of a shared mortgage

There can be a number of drawbacks to a shared mortgage, including:

- Each individual will be given a credit rating and, if anyone has had repayment problems then it may be difficult to obtain a mortgage.
- If one person decides to move it may be difficult unless the others can meet the mortgage payments and the lender is happy with this.
- You must be certain that you can live happily with the other people involved.
- The more people that are involved the more difficult it may be to achieve harmony.
- If the property value decreases you may face the problem of negative equity.

The benefits of a shared mortgage

There are a number of benefits of sharing a mortgage:

- You will be paying half of the monthly cost or less compared to buying the property on your own.
- Sharing allows you to purchase a property that you otherwise would be unable to afford.
- It may allow you to get on the property ladder quicker than on your own.
- You can share in any increase in the value of the property.

SPLIT EQUITY DEALS

One way of getting a bigger property than you can afford is by a split equity deal. Imagine this scenario: a vendor has a property that he has been trying to sell for ages. You as the prospective purchaser have seen the property and have decided that 'this is the one'. The only problem is that you cannot get a mortgage big enough for the property.

The answer is the split equity deal. This is a specific contract whereby you arrange to raise the mortgage on, say, 70% of the cost of the building. However, under the terms of the sale full title passes to you. The vendor under the terms of the contract has a 30% legal second charge against the property (the first charge is held by the mortgage company) with the repayment of the balancing sum payable at a set date in the future. You as the purchaser either arrange a separate savings plan to mature at that date or remortgage or sell the property.

The advantage for you is that you have a conventional mortgage on the property, and you are living in a home which is much bigger than you are actually paying for! The advantage for the vendor is that they have sold the property and have retained a 30% share, which under normal circumstances should rise in value.

For someone who has been sitting for years on a property that cost them little enough in the first place, there is every reason to offer the deal. If you know that you have a vendor in a corner there is every reason to ask for it! Split equity deals can be arranged to suit from 50/50 upwards. However, the mortgage lender has to approve. A competent conveyancing solicitor will be able to draw up the documentation.

BUYING FROM LOCAL AUTHORITIES

Tenants who have lived in a council house for three years or more have a right to buy their house. The discount is calculated on the number of years as a council tenant. The discount can be up to 70% of the value of the property. You do not have to live in the same council house over your qualifying period.

You can arrange to buy the property with a mortgage. Your best advice is to go to an independent financial adviser (IFA) or a mortgage broker. They will help you arrange to buy the house. If you are looking to buy the house in the future then it is worth looking at taking out a savings policy now to pay off the mortgage. An IFA can help advise you on this as well. One very important point to make sure of when buying a council property is to have a good survey done. Many councils have not maintained their houses, and some tenants have not looked after them. It is therefore important to have a good structural survey done and not just a valuation report. Some tenants who have bought their houses have found them to have major structural problems.

There is a useful leaflet *Your right to buy your home* which can be obtained from the Department of the Environment.

HOMEBUY

Another way to get on to the housing ladder even if you may not be able to afford it is via Homebuy. This scheme offers you a loan of 25% of the price of the property you would like to buy. You have to fund the remaining 75%. The 25% loan is interest free but at some point you will have to pay this back at the prevailing market value as set by an independent valuer. The Homebuy scheme is available to any council tenants or housing association tenants, or people on council housing waiting lists, who want to buy their own home. You must, however, be able to meet the following criteria:

- You must be able to cover the extra costs of buying a home such as solicitors' fees.

- You must be in a position where you couldn't afford to buy the property without some help from Homebuy.

- You must be able to get a mortgage in your own right.

- You mustn't be in rent arrears.

- You mustn't be receiving housing benefit or have received it in the last 12 months.

You can find out more about Homebuy by ringing the Housing Corporation, Tel: 020 7393 2000.

You can get advice on mortgages for the Homebuy scheme from an independent financial advisor (IFA).

HOUSING GRANTS

Housing grants are used to improve or renovate properties. It is therefore possible to buy a cheaper property and obtain grants to help improve them. The local authorities administer and give grants, towards which the government contributes the greater part. There are a number of different grants available:

House renovation grant

This is roughly equivalent to what used to be known as an improvement grant. It does not cover second homes, houses built or converted less than ten years ago (unless for disabled facilities), non-essential works, council tenancies or works under the Housing Defects legislation.

Common parts grant

This covers the cost of repairs or improvements to the common parts of buildings containing one or more flats. The landlord or all of the tenants can apply for the grant.

HMO grant

This is a grant for houses with multiple occupation. Only the landlord can apply for this grant.

Disabled facilities grant

This is designed to help make the house of a disabled person more suitable for them to live in. Anyone registered, or registrable, as disabled can apply, whether owner or tenant.

Minor works assistance

This is available only to private sector tenants and owner-occupiers who receive income-related benefits. It covers items such as thermal insulation, adapting or repairing for elderly residents, and the carrying out of repairs to a house in a clearance area.

You can obtain a booklet about all these grants, *House Renovation Grants*, from the Department of the Environment.

Listed buildings

Listed buildings are buildings with special architectural or historic interest. These buildings must not be altered or extended without authorisation from the local planning authority. Grants can be obtained from the local author-ity for essential structural repairs on listed buildings. English Heritage can also make grants for buildings of outstanding interest. The Society for the Protection of Ancient Buildings compiles a list of historic buildings for sale which are in need of sympathetic owners to repair and maintain them.

DSS MORTGAGES

Many part-time workers who receive DSS benefits such as Invalidity or Disability may find it difficult to borrow enough money for a new home. This problem can also affect people who change circumstances. An exist-ing home-owner could lose their job and become reliant on state benefits.

If this person needs to move to a cheaper house to reduce their outgoings they may find it difficult to obtain another mortgage.

Most lenders will not take benefit payments into account when assessing your income. This is because benefit rules often change and there is no guarantee that the benefit levels will remain the same. Lenders will in general look much more favourably at people who can show that they may be able to increase their income in the future. This may be due to the possibility of full- or part-time work, or for other reasons.

It is extremely unusual for lenders to take unemployment benefit into account when assessing income for a mortgage. However, Invalidity and Disability benefits can be considered. Benefits designed to pay for extra services or costs incurred as a result of someone's disability, eg. mobility allowance, are not counted as an income when applying for a mortgage.

If you find yourself on benefits and needing to move you should approach your existing lender first. The existing lender will know your past history well and may be able to help you out. If your existing lender can't help you the best advice is to go to an independent financial adviser (IFA) who will be able to look at thousands of mortgage products.

COUNTY COURT JUDGEMENTS (CCJs) AND ARREARS

Some people who get into financial difficulty can end up with County Court Judgements (CCJs) against them or end up with arrears on their mortgage repayments. A CCJ will remain on a person's record for six years and it is only after that time that their record can be wiped clean. It is often difficult to get a mortgage if you have CCJs. The best advice initially is not to acquire any of them in the first place. However, if you hit financial hardship talk to your mortgage lender and any other company you owe money to quickly. They may be able to help you and enable you to stop getting into arrears or incurring a CCJ.

Many mortgage lenders will automatically refuse borrowers who have arrears or CCJs. However, there are some that will consider them. The lenders that do lend to people with arrears, etc. may charge a higher rate of interest. It is better to talk to an IFA or mortgage broker initially because they may well know the best company to approach first.

The lender will want to look in detail at your CCJs or arrears. They are looking to see if your circumstances and your payment records of loans have improved since your CCJs or arrears. Someone who continues to have bad debt problems is unlikely to get a mortgage.

The lenders may also not be prepared to offer such high loans to values (LTVs) to someone with CCJs or arrears; therefore, they may only offer

75% LTV instead of 95%. This means you may have to find a larger deposit for the house.

There are a number of specialist companies who can help with difficult cases where CCJs and arrears are involved, including:

Kensington Mortgage Company   0800 111020   www.kmc.co.uk

The Mortgage Business   0845 7253253   www.t-m-b-co.uk

Typically these lenders will charge a higher interest rate than the building societies.

You can also contact the following to help with CCJs, arrears, self-employed mortgages and negative equity:

IFAs (independent financial advisers)

Bryan Davies and Company Ltd, 44 High Street, Bridgnorth, Shropshire, WV16 4DX. Tel: 01746 764446.

My brother, Rob Hodson. Tel: 07881 823760.

Mortgage contacts

Charcol. Tel: 0800 718191 or www.charcolonline.co.uk (Charcol are one of the largest mortgage brokers in the country.)

Chase de Vere. Tel: 020 7930 7242 or www.cdvmortgage.co.uk (Chase de Vere are a large mortgage brokers.)

Mortgage Answers. Tel: 0800 195 2485 or www.winterthur-life.co.uk (you can ring the phone number to find your local representative or visit the website.)

IFA promotion. Tel: 01179 711 177 or www.unbiased.co.uk (can give you details of three Independent Financial Advisers near where you live or work.)

NEGATIVE EQUITY

Householders can still suffer from negative equity. Negative equity occurs when the value of the property is less than the mortgage owed on the property, therefore if the owner were to sell the property they would owe the mortgage company money. The property crash of the 1990s was mainly responsible for this when people bought properties and then saw their values tumble.

What can be done if you suffer from negative equity and have to move house? Some people can be forced to move because of any number of events such as new job, divorce or more children. The first thing to do is to contact your existing lender because if the reason is genuine they will often be able to help you. That is provided that your credit rating is good and you have paid your mortgage repayments on time.

Negative equity mortgages

There are a handful of lenders who are offering negative equity mortgages. There are three types of negative equity mortgages.

- The first option is '**let and buy**', which helps home-owners rent out their existing property while providing a second mortgage to buy a new one. Several lenders including the Mortgage Business, Mortgage Express and the Bradford & Bingley and Bristol & West building societies offer let and buy mortgages to both existing and new customers. Let and buy loans are usually available at the variable rate, but can also be fixed. The idea is that when house prices have risen sufficiently the original property can be sold and the mortgage repaid.

- The second option allows the home-owner to sell their existing property and take the outstanding debt to their new house as an unsecured loan. An advantage of this sort of '**mobility mortgage**' scheme is that the interest rate on the loan is usually exactly the same as the mortgage rate rather than a higher personal loan rate. Most lenders will lend up to 135%. Some lenders such as the Woolwich, Halifax and the Cheltenham & Gloucester building societies require a minimum 5% deposit on the property. Others such as the Abbey National require no deposit. The Bank of Scotland scheme requires no deposit and is available on an interest only basis.

- The third option works by securing the outstanding debt left after the sale of the property against the equity in the home of a parent or other family member by means of a remortgage, second mortgage or further advance. This scheme is promoted by the Bradford & Bingley and the Woolwich.

To recap, it is better to approach your existing lender first. If they cannot help then approach your bank, particularly if you have a good credit record with them. If this fails then you can approach the lenders listed below or preferably your IFA.

Mortgage lenders dealing with negative equity

The Mortgage Business	0845 7253253	www.t-m-b-co.uk
Bristol & West	0845 3008000	www.bristol-west.co.uk
Bradford & Bingley	0845 7852852	www.bradford-bingley.co.uk
Mortgage Express	0500 212854	www.mortgage-express.co.uk
Abbey National	0800 555100	www.abbeynational.co.uk
Woolwich	0845 9757575	www.woolwich.co.uk
Halifax	0800 203049	www.halifax.co.uk
Cheltenham & Gloucester	0500 246810	www.cheltglos.co.uk
Bank of Scotland	0845 9812812	www.bankofscotland.co.uk

SELF-EMPLOYED

Self-employed people can find it difficult to obtain a mortgage, particularly in the early years of self-employment. The problem with being self-employed is that there is no employer to confirm their income or payslips to confirm how much is earned. Most lenders can, however, help, although they usually need to see three consecutive years of audited accounts. Audited accounts are those prepared by an accountant and most lenders will only accept accounts prepared by a Chartered Accountant. This probably means that you need to be self-employed for at least four years to have three years of complete accounts.

There are a number of lenders that will look at self-employed people more favourably than this. These include the Bank of Ireland, Capital Home Loans, Bank of Scotland, Centrebank, The Portman Building Society and UCB Homeloans. These lenders will treat self-employed people with only two years' audited accounts as 'full status'.

Limited status mortgages

Another problem that self-employed people face is that they may not be able to borrow all that they need. This is because their taxable income which is shown after deducting expenses and overheads is too low and does not reflect their ability to repay a mortgage. This is where limited status or self-certified mortgages come in. Lenders such as UCB Homeloans, Centrebank and the Mortgage Business do not require accounts or proof of income. The maximum advance on these types of loans is usually 75% or less, but the customer can often borrow more provided their accountant is prepared to sign a questionnaire confirming that they are likely to have sufficient disposable income to meet the payments for the foreseeable future.

Other special deals

The Bank of Scotland will also help those with only one year's accounts. Kensington Mortgage Company will help those who have been self-employed for 12 months and can provide an adequate income certificate from their accountant. Mortgage Express can also help if you have less than three years' accounts. Of course, often your own bank or building society may be able to help you.

Considering a move

If you are considering becoming self-employed and are currently employed then it will be worth considering whether or not you wish to make any property moves in the near future as, if this is the case, then it would be easier to do so while still employed.

Mortgage lenders dealing with the self-employed

UCB Homeloans	0845 9401400	www.ucbhomeloans.co.uk
Legal and General	0500 666555	www.landg.co.uk
The Mortgage Business	0845 7253253	www.t-m-b-co.uk
Bank of Scotland Centrebank	0645 812812	www.bankofscotland.co.uk
Kensington Mortgage Company	0800 111020	www.kmc.co.uk
Bank of Ireland	0800 109010	www.boi-mortgages.co.uk
Portman Building Society	01202 292444	www.portman.co.uk

5

Financial Advice for Mortgages

Taking time to obtain the best financial advice for your mortgage is probably going to be some of the most valuable time spent. A mortgage is likely to be the biggest loan most people ever take out and that means the biggest debt. If you spend time getting good advice it can save you thousands of pounds. Bad advice can cost you dearly, so it is important to get the best advice before you even consider buying a house. Talk to the mortgage advisers first, they can give you an idea of what value property you can afford. You can also talk about the ideas in this book about saving money that may be relevant to you. The big question is where do you start looking for this all important good advice? Financial advice can be obtained from a variety of sources such as banks, building societies, company representatives, mortgage brokers and independent financial advisors (IFAs). The advice can generally be broken down into four categories:

1. mortgage brokers

2. tied agents

3. independent financial advisers

4. direct lenders.

MORTGAGE BROKERS

Mortgage brokers act as the mediator between the lender and the borrower advising on the type of mortgage most suitable. There are thousands of mortgages available some of which are not advertised, and a broker's expert knowledge should narrow the field down to a handful which match your requirements.

● Mortgage brokers specialise purely in mortgage business or insurance products that accompany mortgages.

- They are not allowed to sell you any investment products such as endowments or ISAs unless they are financial advisers as well.

- Typically mortgage brokers are paid once they complete a mortgage for you. Mortgage brokers need to be licensed otherwise lenders will not deal with them. They have to provide lenders with their licence number. Mortgage broking is regulated by the Consumer Credit Act and if you have any complaints you should address them first to the broker and then to the Office of Fair Trading.

If the broker arranges a repayment mortgage for you he may well charge you 1% to 2% of the loan as his charge. If, on the other hand, the mortgage is interest only linked to a savings plan such as an endowment or ISA he should not charge anything as he will earn commission from the plan.

A good broker will give you a choice of mortgages to suit you, with written quotations setting out the payments. You need to go through the quotes carefully and ask if there is anything that you do not understand. Some of the larger mortgage firms are frequently able to arrange special mortgage offers for their clients because of their 'financial muscle'.

There is a list of brokers below.

Mortgage brokers

Charcol	0800 718191	www.charcolonline.co.uk
Chase De Vere	020 7930 7242	www.cdvmortgage.co.uk
Kensington Mortgage Company	0800 111020	www.kmc.co.uk
Ashley Law	0500 104106	
Highfield Financial Planning	01732 353887	
The Financial Surgery	01794 511099	

Mortgage brokers can particularly help those with bad credit histories or self-employed people who may find it difficult to obtain a mortgage. They can also help with negative equity mortgages.

TIED AGENTS

Tied agents usually include the major high street banks and building societies but can include insurance company representatives. A tied agent is linked to just one company and therefore their choice of product is linked to that company. If you approach most of the high street lenders you will usually be recommended their own mortgages, endowments or saving policies if necessary. This automatically limits your choice and you may be missing out on a better mortgage. Some banks and building societies do have independent financial advisers but you will only be directed to these if you ask for them. Tied agents' advice cannot be impartial: any financial solutions that they may offer will be limited by their product range.

The difference between the banks and building societies has become blurred in recent years with some building societies converting to banks. Bank managers are experts in lending and cash flow and they can be a good source of information if you are considering borrowing. You can take advice from your bank manager even if you decide to take the mortgage out elsewhere. Building societies' traditional area of expertise is mortgages and it can often be worth talking to them initially. It is strongly recommended, however, to see a mortgage broker or IFA before you decide to go ahead with a mortgage from a tied agent in case they can offer a better deal for your case.

INDEPENDENT FINANCIAL ADVISER (IFA)

An independent financial adviser (IFA) can sell products of any company giving you a wider choice. They tend to specialise in just mortgages but can also offer you investment advice. They are required by law to give you the best advice for your circumstances. IFAs are regulated by the PIA (Personal Investment Authority) which also regulates tied agents. The PIA insists on certain levels of professional competence and a thorough knowledge of the financial products available and their suitability. This is assessed by a basic examination called the Financial Planning Certificate, which all IFAs must have. Many IFAs will go on to complete more advanced qualifications.

Larger firms of IFAs may well have people who specialise in mortgages, which can be an advantage. The IFAs will often have a computer system linked to all the mortgage offers; this system is updated daily or weekly with the changing mortgages available.

Customer protection

When dealing with IFAs you need to know what sort of protection you have. The Financial Service Act 1986 introduced more protection for the consumer. The system is based on a number of Self-Regulating Organisations (SROs) and Recognised Professional Bodies (RPBs), who now regulate all the different people whom you can go to for money matters. RPBs include the Law Society which governs solicitors and the Institute of Chartered Accountants. SROs include the Personal Investment Authority which governs IFAs and tied agents. It is important that you only go to someone who is a member of an SRO or RPB for any professional advice – this is your first line of defence should anything go wrong.

Knowing what to look for in a good adviser

So, what should you look for in a good adviser? There is a checklist at the end of the chapter which you can use to help you decide. It is a good idea to go to two or three IFAs or, at the very least, ask them a number of questions over the phone. It is important to be able to get on well with your IFA and to trust them. You need to know how long they have been an IFA and how much experience they have. It is better if you can talk to an IFA who specialises in mortgages. One important point that people fail to ask for is the names of two or three customers whom the IFA has dealt with, who would not mind being contacted to check how good the IFA was for them. Mortgage advisors must now have a CeMAP (Certificate in Mortgage Advice and Practice) qualification from November 2002 to advise people in mortgages.

Commission or fee?

IFAs will make money either by earning commission from the policies they recommend to you, or by charging you a fee for their advice. It is important to know which they intend to do. Some IFAs will offer you a choice and this is useful for you because you can choose the best option.

Since 1995 all mortgage advisers whether tied or independent have to disclose exactly how much commission their firm has earned from the recommendation of a product. This will give you an idea as to how much of the premiums will be taken up in commission. This can uncover blatant situations where commission has been the deciding factor in the IFA's recommendation of a product.

However, it is important not to dismiss a product just because it pays a generous commission. Remember that the cheapest product is not always the best! You should discuss this with your IFA and if you are worried that an IFA is recommending products with higher commission then you can always use an IFA who will charge you a fee. In this situation any commission on the product should be returned to you or added to your investment.

Remember that fees can vary greatly so find out exactly what they will be before you start taking advice. It is important to make sure the adviser states when they have started charging you and that they detail their fees in writing.

Two IFAs whom I have personally dealt with are:

Bryan Davies and Company Ltd, 44 High Street, Bridgnorth, Shropshire, WV16 6DX. Tel: 01746 764446.

Rob Hodson. Tel: 07881 823760.

DIRECT LENDERS

There are a number of lenders who only lend direct to the public. IFAs and mortgage brokers may not tell you about them as they often do not pay them commission. These direct lenders will, however, tend not to advise you on whether a repayment or interest only mortgage would be better. They will also generally not be in a position to offer you investment advice.

However, they can often offer you very competitive interest rates, because they have very low overheads compared to the high street lenders. It is therefore often worthwhile ringing them to check what rates they offer. More and more lenders will be setting up direct lending so keep an eye on publications such as *What Mortgage*.

Direct mortgage lenders

Bank of Scotland Direct	0800 810810	www.bankofscotland.co.uk
Direct Line	0845 2468100	www.directline.com/mortgages
Egg	0845 6000290	www.egg.com
First Direct	0845 6100103	www.firstdirect.com
Furness Direct	0800 834312	www.furnessbs.co.uk
Leeds and Holbeck Direct	0800 0725726	www.leeds-holbeck.co.uk
Legal and General	0870 0100338	www.landg.co.uk
Nationwide Direct	0800 302010	www.nationwide.co.uk
Northern Rock Direct	0845 6050500	www.nrock.co.uk
Standard Life Bank	0845 8458450	www.standardlife.com/mortgages

OTHER SOURCES OF INFORMATION

The magazine *What Mortgage* is a very useful source of information on mortgages. It is published each month and is available from most good newsagents. The magazine can offer an independent view of the market-place and it can be a very good idea to look at a few of its issues before you start to look at houses. There are also a number of potentially useful books that you can obtain from the library or buy. The magazine, however, has the advantage of being more up to date on the mortgages available.

Another very useful source of information if you have a fax machine is **Moneyfacts**. You simply dial the number you require and press the start button when you are prompted. You will then get the details you require via the fax. You will, however, be charged for the fax via the phone call.

Moneyfacts numbers

Information	Fax number
Mortgage Selection	0336 400239*
Commercial Mortgages	0336 400237*
Savings Selection	0336 400238*
Low Cost With Profit Endowment	0336 400850
Full Cost With Profit Endowment	0336 400851
Unit Linked Endowment	0336 400852
Level Term Assurance	0336 400853

*Information lines updated daily.   All other lines updated monthly.

Moneyfacts also covers pensions, currency exchange rates, unit trusts, building society rankings, wholesale moneymarket rates, share dealing, loans, National Savings and Income Bonds. The advantage of Moneyfacts is that the information is often updated daily so that you are getting up-to-date information.

Moneyfacts can be contacted on Tel: 01692 500765.

CHEAPER MORTGAGES FROM BROKERS

Many high street lenders may be misleading you by telling you the mortgage loans that they are offering are the cheapest that they offer. They may never tell you that identical loans can be obtained through mortgage brokers up to 0.3% cheaper. Brokers may also be able to negotiate free val-uations and more generous cashbacks. The following examples show you how the brokers can get cheaper rates and save you money:

- Woolwich: 2% discount for 2 years £295 + fee
  Woolwich/Charcol: 2.55% discount for one year then 1.85% discount for another year £99 + fee

- Mortgage Express: 5.99% fixed until 2004 £325 fee
  Mortgage Express/Charcol: 4.99% fixed until 2004 £320 fee

- Bristol and West: 4.75% fixed until 2007
  Bristol and West/Charcol: 4.45% fixed until 2007

- Leeds and Holbeck: 4.29% variable
  Leeds and Holbeck/Charcol: 3.25% variable

These rates will inevitably have changed by the time you read this because mortgages change rapidly. The point is to show you how brokers can arrange cheaper mortgages than you can obtain on the high street. You need to take into account any charges that the broker might make before you make a decision.

CHECKLIST FOR A FINANCIAL ADVISER

- Are they an independent adviser or are they tied?

- Which regulatory body are they authorised by?

- Are they fully authorised?

- Will they refer me to two satisfied customers whom I can ask about their services?

- Do they have professional indemnity insurance? With which company?

- How long have they worked as an adviser, and which companies have they worked for in the last ten years?

- Have they ever been interviewed for any disciplinary matters?

- Do they charge on a fee basis or on a commission basis, or do they do both?

- Will they explain all the charges in detail?

- What is the risk to my money?

- How long has their company been in business?

- Are they competent in all the areas of advice needed?

- Do they offer ongoing advice and support? (Ask for an explanation of the answer.)

- Can I talk freely and easily with the adviser?

- Does the adviser have a CeMAP qualification?

CHECKLIST FOR MORTGAGE ADVICE

- Give the adviser as much information as possible about your current financial position and what type of property you want to buy.

- What mortgage can I afford?

- Which mortgage do they recommend for me?

- Why have they recommended that mortgage?

- What is the interest rate for this mortgage? (Make sure it is the APR.)

- How will the interest rate vary over the course of the loan?

- Will I get a first time buyer discount?

- What will be the payment per £1,000 borrowed?

- What will the following costs be?

  - Stamp Duty

  - legal fees

  - Mortgage Indemnity Premium

  - valuation/survey fees

  - building insurance

  - mortgage arrangement fees/cash backs

  - adviser fees.

- How is interest charged by the lender? (Daily is better than monthly or yearly.)

- What will happen if the interest rate changes?

- Are there any types of insurance that have to be bought as a condition of the loan, eg. house contents or endowments?

- Are there any redemption charges if the mortgage is paid off early?

- What is the lowest current standard rate from a mortgage lender?

- How does the adviser's recommendation compare to the lowest current mortgage rate?

- What is the maximum percentage of the value of the property that I can borrow?

- Can they explain all the mortgage quote fully and show me how much it will cost me?

- How can I reduce the costs of buying the house and the overall mortgage costs of the house?

6

Mortgages

In this chapter we will explain some of the terms associated with mortgages and try and clear up some common questions about mortgages. A mortgage is a loan that is secured on a property. The loan is taken out by you to enable you to buy your house. You are then charged interest on that loan dependent upon the terms you have agreed with the lender. There are two main types of mortgage: **repayment** and **interest only**.

REPAYMENT MORTGAGES

A repayment mortgage is a straightforward mortgage whereby you repay the loan in instalments along with the interest so that by the end of the term you will have paid off your mortgage.

The lender will calculate the mortgage payment so that usually you will pay off the mortgage over a 25-year term. Providing interest rates remain the same these payments will remain the same over the term and at the end of the term your mortgage will be paid off.

During the early years of a repayment mortgage you will mainly be paying interest charges so you will not be paying off much of the capital of the mortgage. During the later years of the mortgage more of your monthly payment will be used to pay off the capital of the mortgage. During the later years the amount of capital you owe on the mortgage will rapidly reduce until your mortgage will be paid off at 25 years (see Figure 3).

Life insurance

Many lenders will also insist that you have a life insurance policy to cover the mortgage in the event of your death. This policy is important if you have dependants as it ensures that the house will be paid for if you die during the term of the mortgage. On the other hand, if you do not have dependants then there is an argument for not having life cover initially but taking it out at a later date when you need to protect your mortgage for your dependants.

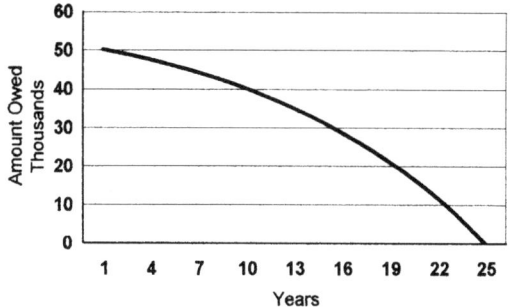

Fig. 3. Repayment mortgage.

Advantages

There are a number of advantages with repayment mortgages.

- Provided you make all your mortgage payments you are guaranteed to pay off your mortgage.

- Repayment mortgages can be taken out over varying lengths of time from 10 years to 35 years or more.

- Once the mortgage is running you can adjust the mortgage if needed, such as increasing or reducing the payments, subject to your lender's approval.

- There are no investment based products attached to repayment mortgages and so there are no commission fees to pay for these products.

- There is less interest to be paid over the lifetime of the mortgage because the capital is being reduced constantly.

- Repayment mortgages can be cheaper than an interest only mortgage with a savings policy.

- You can have decreasing life cover with a repayment mortgage to decrease the cost.

- You can have critical illness protection as a stand alone policy or combined with life cover.

Drawbacks

There are some drawbacks to repayment mortgages.

- Repayment mortgages are not portable and a new loan has to be taken out each time you move.

- As the early repayments have very little effect on the capital, frequent house movers can find themselves with little or no equity in their property after some years of ownership.

- There is no chance of any extra cash lump sum at the end of the mortgage.

- Repayment mortgages do not automatically include life insurance.

It is very important if you move house with a repayment mortgage to try and have a shorter mortgage term of say 20 or 15 years in order to accelerate the repayment process. This will ensure that you pay your mortgage off quickly and thereby save you money.

INTEREST ONLY MORTGAGES

An interest only mortgage is where the borrower only pays interest to the lender and then chooses how to pay back the loan at the end of the term. Endowment, personal pension or ISA mortgages are examples of interest only mortgages. Some lenders will accept interest only mortgages with no savings plan attached.

Each month you will make a mortgage payment for the interest charged on the mortgage loan. You will also make a savings plan payment such as an endowment, ISA or personal pension. If interest rates remain the same these payments will remain the same until the savings plan matures hopefully to pay the mortgage off.

Figure 4 shows how the savings plan grows in value in the case of an endowment. As you can see, during the early years the endowment grows slowly. In the later years the growth increases owing to the effects of compound interest. The endowment is designed to build up a sufficient tax free cash lump sum to pay the mortgage off at 25 years, in this case £40,000.

Advantages

There are a number of advantages of interest only mortgages.

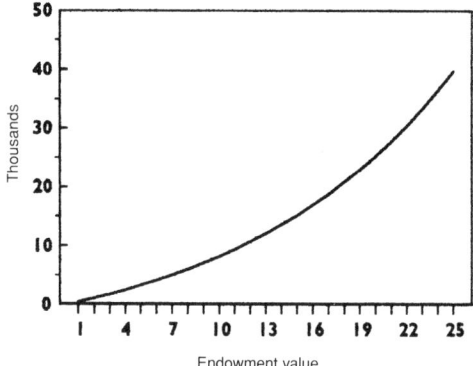

Fig. 4. Endowment mortgage.

● You have the freedom to choose how to pay off an interest only mortgage, for example, using an ISA, personal pension or endowment.

● You can have an extra cash lump sum if your savings plan performs well at the end of your mortgage.

● You can stop or take money out of your savings plan if you hit financial hardship, subject to the approval of the lender.

● If you move house frequently, an interest only mortgage can be better than a repayment mortgage.

● You can increase your savings plan to pay your mortgage off quicker.

● You can pay some capital off your mortgage as and when you want to, provided that there are no redemption penalties.

● An interest only mortgage is relatively flexible.

Disadvantages

There are a number of disadvantages to interest only mortgages.

● If your savings plan performs badly you will have to make up the shortfall.

● You will be charged more in interest charges over the lifetime of the mortgage than with a repayment mortgage.

● If you take out a savings plan you will be charged a commission.

● Some lenders can insist on certain policies such as endowments.

METHODS OF CHARGING INTEREST

Interest on both interest-only and repayment mortgages can be charged in a variety of ways, the most common being as follows.

Variable interest mortgage

This means that the interest rate changes when the lender reduces or increases their lending rate. If you take out a fixed or capped rate mortgage (see below), the interest rate will usually revert to a variable rate after the fixed or capped rate has finished, unless, for example, you have a 25-year fixed rate.

You can often get discounted rates or cash back incentives on variable rate mortgages. The majority of discounts will last a year or two. There are discounts available for longer but a longer period usually means a smaller discount.

There can, however, be arrangement fees charged for discount rates or cashback mortgages. There can also be early redemption penalties of usually around three months of interest on these special mortgages. Therefore if you are forced to move home early you could be charged three months' interest. The same can apply on early full or part redemption.

Capped rates

This type of mortgage provides a cap on the level to which the interest rate on the mortgage can rise. The mortgage is capped rather than fixed so that the repayments can move up and down below the level of the cap depending on what interest rates are doing generally.

In principle a capped rate provides the security of a fixed rate with the speculative advantage of a variable rate mortgage. So if, for example, you have a capped rate of 5.5% over 2 years and the lender's rate rises to 6% or above, your interest rate will stay at 5.5%. If your lender's rate falls below 5.5% to say 5%, your rate will go down to 5%.

Some capped rates have a **collar** which works in the same way to limit how low the mortgage can go down. So in the example above, if your mortgage was capped at 5.5% and collared at 4%, if the mortgage rate was 6% you would pay 5.5% and if the mortgage rate went down to 3.5% you would pay 4%. Therefore your mortgage could fluctuate between 5.5% and 4%.

- The capped rate is usually only in place for a specified period of time, usually from 1 to 5 years. The mortgage will usually revert to the lender's standard rate once the capped rate has finished. It is therefore very important to **check what will happen when your capped rate finishes**. Some lenders will offer very attractive capped rates to attract you initially but when the capped rate finishes they may charge you a high variable rate of interest compared to other lenders.

- Capped rates may often have **arrangement fees** associated with them. There can also be **compulsory insurances** such as buildings or contents insurance. These can make the mortgage more expensive.

- You must also check if there are any **early redemption penalties** if you redeem your mortgage or move house. Penalties of three to six months of interest payments are quite common with capped mortgages. Redemption penalties can extend beyond the capped rate period so make sure to check.

- Some lenders will allow the capped rate to be **portable** and thereby move the mortgage if you buy another house. A portable capped rate is a very useful feature so check this with your lender.

You have to decide with the help of an IFA or financial adviser what mortgage rate you are looking for. It depends on how you see the mortgage rates moving and your own personal finances. In general you can choose a very low capped rate for a short time or a rate that is capped at a higher level but for a longer period of time. Make sure you look at the extra charges involved and the variable rate after the capped rate finishes, not just the attractive capped rate.

Fixed rate mortgages

The mortgage lender can offer you a fixed rate mortgage where the interest rate is fixed at a specified rate for a set period of time. Therefore if, for example, you fix the rate at 5.5% for 2 years your mortgage payments would stay at 5.5% for 2 years irrespective of what happens to mortgage rates. After your fixed rate has finished the mortgage rate will usually revert to your lender's standard variable rate. This is unless your lender will allow you to change to another capped or fixed rate.

- The main **advantage** of fixed rates is that repayments will remain exactly the same so that it is easy to budget for them. This is particularly useful if your finances are tight and you are on a restricted budget.

- Over the past ten years the average mortgage interest rate has been about 9%; over the last 25 years it has been about 10%. Therefore if you can arrange long-term fixed rates below these levels they may well be worth looking at closely.

- The **drawbacks** of fixed rate mortgages are that **arrangement fees** are often charged.

- There are also often **redemption penalties** of three to six months worth of interest payments if you pay off or redeem your mortgage early. These redemption penalties may extend beyond the fixed rate period so make sure to check.

- A number of lenders will allow you to move your fixed rate if you buy another house but it is important to check this first before you arrange your fixed rate mortgage.

- Another disadvantage of fixed rates is that your mortgage rate will not go down if mortgage rates go below the rate you fix at. There is also the possibility that mortgage rates could go much higher than your fixed rate. Then when your fixed rate finishes your mortgage payments would rise markedly which could lead to financial problems if you don't budget for the rise. If you wish to know what your mortgage payments will be with certainty you can fix your mortgage for a long time, up to 25 years.

- It is best to take the advice of an IFA on fixed mortgages.

APR (ANNUAL PERCENTAGE RATE)

APR is a yardstick that you can use to compare borrowing. It is a single figure representing the annual cost of a loan when interest and fees are taken into account. It was introduced in the Consumer Credit Act of 1974 to help consumers understand the true cost of borrowing. APR provides an accurate way of comparing the true cost of borrowing and therefore a way to compare mortgage loans. The higher the APR the more the borrower will have to pay. Therefore by looking at the APR you should be able to determine whether or not you are getting a good deal.

To calculate the APR of a mortgage, lenders must take into account any changes in the interest rate during the course of the mortgage term. Lenders also have to include any compulsory insurances which cover repayment of the loan in the event of death, illness, unemployment or invalidity. This means that any extra policies that the lender requires are taken into account when they calculate the APR. Therefore APR will give you a useful tool to compare mortgages. You must, however, not use APR alone to decide which is the best mortgage for you.

CAT MORTGAGES

CAT standards have been brought in by the government. CAT stands for Charges, Access and Terms so that CAT mortgages should have fair charges and clear terms and conditions. All CAT mortgages must have interest charged on a daily basis, a clear breakdown of charges and no fees paid by borrowers to brokers. CAT mortgages should also be fairly priced. In the case of variable rate loans the interest rate should be no more than 2% above the Bank of England base rate. Existing borrowers can take advantage of CAT mortgages.

So should you consider a CAT mortgage? It is well worth asking an IFA about CAT standard mortgages and whether they will suit your circumstances. CAT mortgages are certainly clear mortgages that shouldn't give you too many surprises. The best advice, though, is to get good advice from an IFA.

UNDERSTANDING THE MORTGAGE QUOTE

The mortgage quote can often seem a complicated piece of paper that many people fail to understand. It is important to take a little time to understand it because it could save you a vast amount of money. We will show you a typical mortgage quote and what it means and what to look for.

The example in Figure 5 shows the important points in a mortgage quote. The format of mortgage quotes can be different but they contain all the information you need to compare mortgages. If, when you look at quotes, there is anything you do not understand then ask the financial adviser to explain. Remember that it is your money. One of the most important questions to ask is how can you reduce the total amount that you will pay for the mortgage?

Total amount requested

This details the mortgage amount that you have requested to borrow. In this case it is £80,000. You need to ensure that this is the correct amount that you need to borrow. It is also important to note that the less that you borrow the less you will be charged in interest. It is often worthwhile asking for a quote of a few thousand pounds cheaper to see what savings you could make. The less you borrow the cheaper your house will cost you over the mortgage term.

Total amount requested	£80,000.00
Total amount of interest	£71,713.00
Charges and fees	nil
Total charge for credit	£71,713.00
Total amount repayable	£151,713.00
To be repaid monthly by 300 payments of	£505.71
Annual percentage rate (APR)	6.0%
Charges and fees:	
Description of charge	*Amount*
Valuation fee	£255 (estimate)
Solicitor's fees	nil
Arrangement fee	nil
Higher loan to value access fee	nil
Total carried to charges and fees	nil

Fig. 5. Example repayment mortgage quote.

Total amount of interest

This shows the total amount of interest charged. When you are comparing mortgages it is very important to look for the mortgage that charges you the lowest amount of interest possible. It is important to get a number of mortgage quotes and compare them. Ask for a number of different types of quotes and notice how the interest charged varies, such as:

● a mortgage over a 25-year term

● a mortgage over a 24-year term

● a mortgage over a 20-year term

● a smaller mortgage of a few thousand pounds less

● paying your mortgage every 4 weeks, 2 weeks or weekly

● increasing your mortgage payment each year.

Above all it is important for you to understand how the interest you are charged for your mortgage can be reduced. Ask the IFA or financial adviser to explain any questions you may have and show you how you can save interest charges. In this example, as you can see, the interest charged is

£71,713 which is nearly the same as the £80,000 you are borrowing. That is why it is so important to try to reduce the interest that you will be charged. An important point to note is that lenders reserve the right in the future to be less competitive on their mortgage interest rates. Therefore you should review your mortgage every few years to check how competitive your mortgage rate is. If it is no longer competitive then look to negotiate a reduced rate with your existing lender or remortgage.

Charges and fees

This shows what charges will be paid for the mortgage. You need to look for a mortgage with the lowest charges. If there are charges make sure you know what the charges are for and ask why they are being charged. Then you can ask if there is any way of reducing them or getting rid of them. If the charges are high it may well be worth looking at other lenders. Remember that you can often negotiate to reduce these charges because the mortgage business is very competitive.

Total charge for credit

This takes into account the interest charged and the charges. You are looking for the lowest total charge possible. As said earlier, get a number of quotes.

Total amount repayable

This shows the total amount that would be repayable for the loan. This is the most important part of the quote. This shows you the total cost of the mortgage. It is often a fright to see how much the mortgage will eventually cost you. It is important to look at this carefully and find out how you can reduce this. In this example, for £80,000 the total cost is £151,713 which is nearly double the initial £80,000. Here are a few ways you could reduce this:

- Reduce the term of the mortgage.

- Reduce the amount you borrow.

- Reduce the interest rate by borrowing from a cheaper lender.

- Reduce the costs by negotiating or choosing a cheaper lender.

- Also ask your IFA or financial adviser if there are any other ways to reduce the total amount that you will pay for the mortgage.

To be repaid monthly

This details the way the mortgage will be paid and for how long. It is important to look at this and make sure you are happy with the figures and ask yourself a number of questions:

- Can I afford these payments?

- Can I afford the mortgage payments if interest rates go up?

- Would payments made every 4 weeks, 2 weeks or weekly suit me better and save me money?

- Can I afford these payments if my income reduces; for example, loss of earnings or retirement?

Annual percentage rate (APR)

This shows you the APR interest rate of the mortgage. This gives you a good guide to how competitive the interest rate is. Do not rely solely on APR to choose a mortgage. A mortgage is like a suit of clothes in that it will suit one person well but not another.

Summary checklist

- Ask for several mortgage quotes and compare them.

- Ask the financial adviser to explain anything that you don't understand.

- Ask how you can reduce the total amount you will pay for the mortgage.

MORTGAGE REPAYMENTS TABLE

The table in Figure 6 can be used to help you to calculate the approximate monthly cost of a mortgage. It is very useful to work out figures for mortgages of different lengths or for different amounts. The table shows the cost per month of borrowing £1,000 for repayment mortgages over ten to 30 years and in the final column the cost of an interest only mortgage not taking into account any investment product.

To show you how to use the table here are some examples:

- A £60,000 repayment mortgage over 25 years at 5.75% = 60 × £6.36 = £381.60 a month.

- A £60,000 repayment mortgage over 15 years at 5.75% = 60 × £8.44 = £506.40 a month.

Rate	10 years	15 years	20 years	25 years	30 years	Interest only
4.50%	£10.53	£7.76	£6.41	£5.62	£5.12	£3.75
4.75%	£10.66	£7.89	£6.55	£5.77	£5.27	£3.96
5.00%	£10.79	£8.03	£6.69	£5.91	£5.42	£4.17
5.25%	£10.92	£8.16	£6.83	£6.06	£5.58	£4.38
5.50%	£11.06	£8.30	£6.97	£6.21	£5.73	£4.58
5.75%	£11.19	£8.44	£7.12	£6.36	£5.89	£4.79
6.00%	£11.32	£8.58	£7.27	£6.52	£6.05	£5.00
6.25%	£11.46	£8.72	£7.41	£6.67	£6.22	£5.21
6.50%	£11.59	£8.86	£7.56	£6.83	£6.38	£5.42
6.75%	£11.73	£9.01	£7.71	£6.99	£6.55	£5.63
7.00%	£11.86	£9.15	£7.87	£7.15	£6.72	£5.83
7.25%	£12.00	£9.29	£8.02	£7.31	£6.88	£6.04
7.50%	£12.14	£9.44	£8.17	£7.48	£7.06	£6.25
7.75%	£12.28	£9.59	£8.33	£7.64	£7.23	£6.46
8.00%	£12.42	£9.74	£8.49	£7.81	£7.40	£6.67
8.25%	£12.56	£9.88	£8.65	£7.97	£7.58	£6.88
8.50%	£12.70	£10.04	£8.81	£8.14	£7.75	£7.09
8.75%	£12.84	£10.19	£8.97	£8.31	£7.93	£7.29
9.00%	£12.99	£10.34	£9.13	£8.48	£8.11	£7.50

Fig. 6. Mortgage repayments table.

- A £50,000 interest only mortgage at 5.75% = 50 × £4.79 = £239.50 a month.

The figures are approximately correct but the actual figures from a lender can vary slightly owing to the way the lender charges interest. Therefore for a precise monthly figure always get a quote from the lender.

This table is very useful to show you the cost of mortgages. Play around with the table and work out some of the following scenarios for your mortgage:

- A mortgage for a few thousand pounds cheaper; for example, £69,000 and £67,000.

- A mortgage over a shorter term; for example, 25 years and 20 years.

- Work out the total cost; for example, a £60,000 repayment mortgage at 5.75% over 25 years = £381.60 a month = £381.60 × 12 × 25 = £114,480 over 25 years.

Always remember that you are trying to reduce the total cost of your mortgage.

MORTGAGE LENDERS ON THE INTERNET

A wide range of financial services are now available on the Internet. These include help with picking your new property, arranging your mortgage or even house insurance. Homes are now listed in all countries and you can have a guided tour around them. There are a number of lenders on the Internet now and soon you will be able to arrange a mortgage via the Internet. Some lenders help visitors on their pages. The Alliance and Leicester provides electronic programs to work out the monthly cost of your mortgage repayments. Legal and General also have a mortgage calculator and a form on screen which you can fill in for a financial planner to contact you at a convenient time.

Shopping on the Internet will become part of normal life soon. You will be able to buy all financial products and probably get advice as well. The Internet will become the biggest and busiest shopping arcade in existence.

The basic equipment you need to get connected to the Internet is a modem, telephone line and computer. Once you have signed up with a service provider you can surf the Net for the cost of a local call. When you are online you will need one of the 'search engines'. These are computer programs that sort through millions of websites on the Internet and create mini-directories by subject matter. One of the easiest search engines is Yahoo. You can reach this page by going to www.yahoo.com. Once you have contacted the Yahoo page you can type in the area that interests you, for example mortgages, and Yahoo will provide you with links to websites across the Internet. Here are some useful Internet addresses:

Lender	*Address*
Abbey National	www.abbeynational.co.uk
Alliance and Leicester	www.alliance-leicester.co.uk/mortgage
Barclays Bank	www.barclays.co.uk

Cheltenham & Gloucester	www.cheltglos.co.uk
Halifax	www.halifax.co.uk
Legal and General	www.legal-and-general.co.uk
Midland Bank	www.midlandbank.co.uk
Nationwide	www.nationwide.co.uk
NatWest	www.natwestgroup.com/nwukhome.html

Other useful websites

Moneynet	www.moneynet.co.uk
Express UK Mortgages	www.ip7.co.uk
Financial Information Net Directory	www.find.co.uk
First Property Search	www.first-mortgage.co.uk
Home Builder (self-build information)	www.gold.net
Homesellers Direct	www.homesellers-direct.co.uk
PropertyNet Buyers Guide	www.god.co.uk
Asserta (mortgages and houses)	www.assertahome.co.uk
Yahoo loan	www.loan.yahoo.com
The Motley Fool (financial advice)	www.fool.co.uk
Virgin Money	www.virginmoney.com
Intelligent Finance	www.if.com
FT Your Money	www.ftyourmoney.com

Moneynet is a UK mortgage site that provides free access to over 1,200 mortgages from 90 lenders. The site is updated daily and is independently owned so that it is not biased. There are 4 broad categories available on the site:

1. Residential – standard mortgages.
2. Flexible Lifestyle mortgages – for mortgages which offer flexible features such as drawdown facilities, payment breaks and the ability to overpay.

3. Arrears, CCJs and Non-Status – mortgages for more difficult cases that not every lender will cover.

4. Buy to Let – mortgages for the purchase of properties to let.

All you have to do is press the search button and fill in the following details:

- the value of the property

- the amount of the mortgage

- your salary details

- whether you are a first time buyer, previous purchaser or remortgaging

- you can specify the type of mortgage you want; for example, fixed, capped, discount or variable.

Moneynet does make the point that the lowest rate is not necessarily the most suitable product for you and you should consider the other terms of the mortgage. Moneynet also has answers to the most frequently asked questions and a glossary of technical terms and a mortgage calculator.

TELETEXT AND CEEFAX

Teletext and Ceefax both carry a lot of information on mortgages and other financial advice. They provide you with details of first time buyer mortgages, discount mortgages, fixed rate mortgages and capped rates. It is well worth looking at these pages because they are updated very regularly. They can help you keep up to date on any latest rate changes.

- Teletext is on Channel 4 on page 545.

- Ceefax is on BBC2 on page 250.

7

Reducing Mortgage Costs

There are three golden rules to reduce your mortgage costs:

- borrow as little as possible

- borrow at the cheapest interest rate

- reduce your mortgage term to the minimum.

BORROW AS LITTLE AS POSSIBLE

If you borrow less using a mortgage then you will pay less in interest charges. The table in Figure 7 will show you the costs of borrowing.

Total amount borrowed	Monthly cost of a repayment mortgage at 5.75%	Total cost over 25 years
£60,000	£381.60	£114,480
£50,000	£318.00	£95,400
£40,000	£254.40	£76,320
£30,000	£190.80	£57,240
£20,000	£127.20	£38,160
£10,000	£63.60	£19,080

Fig. 7. Costs of borrowing.

As you can see from the table, if you borrow less you will pay less for your mortgage and therefore less for your house. There are a number of ways you can reduce the amount of money you need to borrow:

- buy your house cheaper by buying it at auction

- build your own house

- save a larger deposit towards your house

- use any unexpected windfall to reduce the amount you borrow on your mortgage

- negotiate a cheaper purchase price for your house.

Many people fall into the trap of borrowing more than they need because it seems so cheap. To borrow £1,000 at 5.75% with a repayment mortgage over 25 years only costs £6.36 per month. Therefore many people borrow more than they need to buy larger houses. Remember that every extra £1,000 you borrow on a mortgage will cost you £1,908 in the above examples.

BORROW AT THE CHEAPEST RATE

There are three main factors which can help you to borrow at the cheapest mortgage rate:

- choose the cheapest mortgage lender

- choose a lender that charges interest on a daily basis

- negotiate a cheaper mortgage rate.

Choose the cheapest mortgage lender

There are thousands of mortgage lenders in the marketplace. Many smaller lenders or direct lenders will charge lower mortgage interest rates than the main high street lenders. It is vital to get good advice from an IFA to help you to choose a mortgage lender that can offer you a low interest rate. The table in Figure 8 shows you how savings of 0.25% on the mortgage interest rate can save you money over the long term.

As you can see from the table, a reduction of 0.5% from 6% to 5.5% would save you £5,580. Many people have saved 0.5% or more by concentrating on the following:

- get good advice from an IFA

- look at direct lenders

- look at mutual building societies

- look at small local building societies.

Repayment mortgage of £60,000 over 25 years at:	Monthly cost	Total cost over 25 years
5%	£354.60	£106,380
5.25%	£363.60	£109,080
5.5%	£372.60	£111,780
5.75%	£381.60	£114,480
6.0%	£391.20	£117,360

Fig 8. Interest rate savings.

Contacts

Direct Line	0845 2468100	www.directline.com/mortgages
Egg	0845 6000290	www.egg.com
First Direct	0845 6100103	www.firstdirect.com
Furness Direct	0800 834312	www.furnessbs.co.uk
Leeds and Holbeck Direct	0800 0725726	www.leeds-holbeck.co.uk
Legal and General	0870 0100338	www.landg.co.uk
Nationwide Direct	0800 302010	www.nationwide.co.uk
Northern Rock Direct	0845 6050500	www.nrock.co.uk
Standard Life Bank	0845 8458450	www.standardlife.com/mortgages

What Mortgage magazine does a survey each year of the cheapest lenders. The major high street lenders often do poorly in the survey. Many of the direct lenders and smaller lenders do well because their overheads are lower. If you can look at their annual survey it makes very interesting reading.

Choose a lender that charges interest on a daily basis

Britain's borrowers could be being overcharged £73 billion pounds in unnecessary interest charges over the next 25 years because of lenders' outdated computer systems. Findings show that typical borrowers with a £51,000 mortgage will pay £13,680 too much interest over the life of their mortgages because of the old-fashioned way interest is applied. This could mean they are paying an extra £45 a month in interest charges.

Many lenders charge interest yearly and in arrears. Therefore they take no account of repayments credited by a customer during the previous 12 months. These lenders are getting a 12-month interest free loan from you, the borrower. Annual calculations are based on the outstanding balance on the first day of each year in question and do not take into account payments during that year.

Daily calculations of interest take account of every payment, adjusting the debt every 24 hours and substantially reducing the overall interest paid. The lenders that charge you interest on a daily basis include a lot of the newer mortgage lenders such as Direct Line, Legal and General, Bank of Scotland Direct and Standard Life. The only advantage of annual interest calculations is for any borrower who falls into arrears. The majority of borrowers could benefit from being charged on a daily basis.

Lenders such as the Bank of Ireland work out interest payments on a monthly basis (called monthly rests). This method of monthly rests will reduce the payments by about 0.1% on a normal repayment mortgage compared to an annual system. Therefore it is very important to know how your interest is charged.

The best option for you is to be charged on a daily basis unless you think you may go into arrears. This is one of the reasons lenders such as Direct Line are offering low standard variable mortgage rates because they charge interest daily. Therefore whenever possible try to choose a lender that charges interest on a daily basis unless the lender is offering a very cheap mortgage rate.

Negotiate a cheaper mortgage rate

Many people forget that you can negotiate with your current lender to reduce your interest rate. Many people have already done this. The best way to do this is to look at remortgaging and find a cheaper lender and get a quote from them. Then use this quote to go back to your current lender and ask them to match or improve on this. As you have seen earlier, a 0.5% saving can be worth thousands of pounds. An IFA can help you with a remortgage quote and find a cheaper lender. If your current lender will not reduce your mortgage rate you can consider remortgaging (discussed in Chapter 9).

REDUCE YOUR MORTGAGE TERM TO THE MINIMUM

There are a number of ways you can reduce your mortgage term and reduce the cost of your mortgage. You can:

- increase your monthly mortgage payment
- pay a lump sum off your mortgage

- pay your mortgage more often
- start a savings policy before you start your mortgage
- increase a savings policy
- take out a flexible mortgage or a current account mortgage.

Increase your monthly mortgage payment

You can increase your mortgage payment to pay your mortgage off sooner. You will need to check with your mortgage lender how your overpayments will reduce your mortgage. It is very important to check how your lender charges interest on your mortgage. If your lender charges interest on an annual basis on 31 December each year, any overpayments you make will not reduce your mortgage until 31 December. Therefore you will be much better off saving your overpayments in a building society account and earning interest on them. Then make a lump sum overpayment off your mortgage just before 31 December. If your lender charges interest on a daily basis or monthly basis then your overpayments will have a much quicker effect on reducing your mortgage. The table in Figure 9 is supplied by

Monthly overpayment on a £90,000 mortgage at 5.2%	Interest saved	Time saving in years and months off the term
£50	£17,744	4 years 7 months
£100	£25,359	7 years 2 months
£150	£30,998	9 years 2 months
£200	£35,359	10 years 9 months

Source: virginone.com

Fig. 9. Overpayments to reduce mortgage term.

Increase in your monthly mortgage payment each year	Interest saved	Time saved in years and months off term of mortgage
1%	£10,764.38	3 years and 10 months
2%	£17,823.13	6 years and 3 months

Source: Clydesdale Bank

Fig. 10. Effects of increasing monthly repayments.

Virgin One will show you how overpayments can reduce your mortgage term and save you money over a 25-year term.

The table assumes that the mortgage interest remains the same throughout the mortgage and that overpayments are not withdrawn. The examples are for repayment mortgages. You can also increase your monthly mortgage payment gradually over time to pay your mortgage off sooner. Many people get a pay rise each year and if part of this is used to increase mortgage payments, money can be saved.

The table in Figure 10 is based on a 25-year repayment mortgage of £90,000 at 5.9%. It is assumed that the interest rate remains the same throughout the mortgage. The table shows the effect of increasing your monthly mortgage payment by 1% or 2% each year. As you can see, small increases in your mortgage payment can make a big difference.

Pay a lump sum off your mortgage

You can pay lump sums off your mortgage to save money on the cost of your mortgage. You will be getting a return on your money equivalent to the mortgage rate. Therefore if you are paying 5.2% on your mortgage you will effectively be getting a return of 5.2% on any lump sum payment you make into the mortgage. You will also not be taxed on this payment so your return will be higher compared to keeping your money in a taxable building society or bank account. Therefore if you have any cash lump sums earning a low level of interest it can be well worth looking at paying part of your mortgage off. Remember to check when your mortgage lender charges interest and pay any lump sum in at the most advantageous time to reduce your mortgage.

The table in Figure 11 shows how you can save money by making lump sum overpayments. The example shows a £90,000 mortgage at 5.2% over 25 years.

Pay your mortgage more often

Most lenders will only allow you to pay for your mortgage once a month. There are, however, lenders that will allow you to pay your mortgage weekly or fortnightly. By paying your mortgage more frequently you can pay your mortgage off more quickly and save money.

The table in Figure 12 is based on a 25-year mortgage of £90,000 at 5.9%. It is assumed that interest rates remain the same throughout the term of the mortgage.

It can suit many people who are paid weekly or fortnightly to pay their mortgage in this manner. As you can see here, it will save you money as well.

Lump sum overpayment	Interest saved	Time saving in years and months off term
£5,000	£17,649	3 years 6 months
£10,000	£26,712	5 years 8 months
£15,000	£34,359	7 years 7 months
£20,000	£40,830	9 years 5 months

Source: virginone.com

Fig. 11. Lump sum overpayments.

Frequency of mortgage payment	Interest saved compared to monthly payments	Time saving in years and months off term
Fortnightly	£7,086.46	1 year and 11 months
Weekly	£6,514.62	1 year and 9 months

Source: Clydesdale Bank

Fig. 12. Paying your mortgage more often.

Start a savings policy before you start your mortgage

Many people do not realise that you can start a savings policy to pay your mortgage off before you start your mortgage. If you know that you are going to take out a mortgage in the future you can save a lot of money by starting a savings plan before your mortgage. You can start an endowment, ISA or pension in advance of your mortgage. Starting a savings policy before a mortgage is not normally recommended by IFAs because the regulatory bodies frown upon it. You can, however, decide to do this yourself by instructing an IFA. Always be guided by the advice of a good IFA. The table in Figure 13 will show you how much you can save on a £60,000 interest only mortgage at 5.75% that would be paid over 25 years.

As you can see, starting a savings plan before you start your mortgage will help you to pay off your mortgage more quickly and save money. It is important to talk to an IFA for advice and start a flexible savings plan. The savings plan needs to be flexible so that if you decide to take out a larger mortgage you can increase the savings plan to pay off a larger mortgage. Also make sure that you don't take out life insurance until you need it to

Start of savings plan before your mortgage	Saving in mortgage costs
1 month	£381.60
12 months	£4,579.20
24 months	£9,158.40

Fig. 13. Starting a savings policy before your mortgage.

cover yourself and any dependants. In many cases you can start a savings policy and then take out life insurance at a later date.

Increase a savings policy

You can at any stage either increase a savings policy or take out an additional savings policy to pay off your mortgage more quickly. You will need to check a number of important details first with the company that deals with your savings policy or get an IFA to check for you:

- Check when your policy matures.
- Is your policy a with-profits or unit linked policy?
- Find out if you can increase your policy.
- Find out if you can take out an additional top-up policy.

If your policy is a with-profits policy it is usually best to let it run to its full term because you will get a terminal bonus which can increase the return of the policy quite markedly. If your policy is a unit linked policy and you can increase the policy or top it up you can look at increasing your policy. ISAs are very tax efficient flexible savings policies that can be increased to pay your mortgage off more quickly. The table in Figure 14 shows how you can pay your mortgage off more quickly and save money by paying more into a savings policy. The table is based on an £80,000 mortgage at 5.75% interest.

As you can see if you could increase your ISA from £137 to £171 a month, an increase of £34 a month, you could save £9,751.20. If you choose a flexible savings plan such as an ISA you can make increases to your policy gradually each year. Many people get a pay rise each year and if you could use some of this to increase your savings policy you will save money on the cost of your mortgage. Always check with an IFA on the best way in which you can use your savings policy to pay off your mortgage

Term of the ISA	Monthly cost of the ISA	Monthly mortgage cost	Total cost over the whole term
25 years	£137.00	£383.20	£156,060
22 years	£171.00	£383.20	£146,308.80
20 years	£199.00	£383.20	£139,728
15 years	£307.00	£383.20	£124,308

Fig. 14. Increasing your savings policy.

sooner. Many advisers may advise you to increase your mortgage payments before considering increasing a savings policy. You need to be aware of the risks. Increasing your mortgage payment to pay your mortgage off sooner is considered low risk. In the case of savings policies with-profits endowments are considered low to medium risk. Unit linked endowments are considered medium to high risk. Savings policies based on stocks and shares are considered medium to high risk. An IFA can give you a good idea of the risk of any policy you may be considering. Always take on board the advice of a good IFA.

Take out a flexible mortgage or current account mortgage

Flexible mortgages and current account mortgages are becoming more popular and for good reason. These types of mortgage offer you a lot more flexibility in our changing economic times. They can offer the following features:

- You can make overpayments to pay your mortgage off more quickly.

- You can borrow these overpayments back at a later date.

- You can pay on a flexible basis, for example, 10 payments a year, weekly or fortnightly.

- If you have made overpayments you can underpay or have a break from your mortgage payment.

- Daily calculation of interest.

- Current account facilities.

Flexible mortgages give you the freedom to pay your mortgage off more quickly in a number of ways. We will use an example of the Virgin One account to show you how this can work. The Virgin One account is a current account based mortgage. Suppose your finances look like this:

Annual income	£35,000
Borrowings	£70,000
Savings	£5,000
House value	£120,000

- If you have a traditional 25-year repayment mortgage with interest charged at 5.2%, the monthly cost would be £417.42.

- If you have a Virgin One account, based on the same term, charged at the same interest rate and costing the same amount each month, and you pay in your monthly income, spending it evenly over the month, you'll repay your borrowing 7 months early, saving you £3,331.

- If you leave a little extra in the account as well – say £50 a month – you'll pay off your borrowing 5 years 2 months early, saving £14,394.

- If you also put in your £5,000 savings at the start, your total saving will be £22,384 in interest and you'll repay your borrowing 7 years 6 months early. And remember you've still got instant access to the savings.

As you can see from these examples, you can save a lot of money with a current account mortgage. There are many flexible mortgages on the market now and the list is growing. The best advice is to talk to an IFA about all the options.

Flexible mortgages

Abbey National	0800 555100	www.abbeynational.co.uk
Clydesdale Bank	0800 419000	www.cbonline.co.uk
Egg	08456 000290	www.egg.com
Legal and General Bank	0870 0100338	www.landg.co.uk
Standard Life Bank	0845 8458450	www.standardlifebank.com/ mortgages
Virgin Direct*	08456 000001	www.virginone.com
Yorkshire Bank	0800 202122	www.ybonline.co.uk
Yorkshire Building Society	0845 1200100	www.ybs.co.uk
Coventry Building Society	08457 665522	www.covbsoc.co.uk
Hinckley and Rugby Building Society	0800 774499	www.hrbs.co.uk

*current account mortgage

CHECKLIST

- Borrow as little as possible.
- Buy your home at auction.
- Build your own home.
- Negotiate a purchase price on your home.
- Pay a larger deposit on your home.
- Borrow at the cheapest mortgage rate.
- Choose a lender that charges low interest rates.
- Consider a remortgage.
- Negotiate a lower interest rate.
- Choose a lender that charges interest on a daily basis.
- Increase your monthly mortgage payment.
- Pay a lump sum off your mortgage.
- Pay your mortgage more often; for example, weekly or fortnightly.
- Start a savings policy before your mortgage starts.
- Increase your savings policy to pay your mortgage off more quickly.
- Take out a flexible or current account mortgage.

8

Reducing Your Ongoing Home Costs

In this chapter we will be looking at saving money on the costs involved in your home as you can save a surprising amount. I will show you how I will save £4,200 on home insurance and £3,000 on life insurance, and how I can get a 30% return on my money. I will look at three main areas:

- home buildings and contents insurance

- home energy costs

- life insurance costs.

HOME BUILDINGS AND CONTENTS INSURANCE

It is important to shop around for buildings insurance, particularly by using telebrokers. Some telebrokers have offered to give a quote cheaper than the cheapest quote you can find elsewhere at promotional times. When you have found your cheapest quote, go back to one or two telebrokers and see if they will match or beat your quote. A telephone call could save you some more money. Direct Line claims that home owners are paying over a third more for their cover than is necessary if you stay with your mortgage lender for your house insurance.

No two insurance companies will ever give the same quote for the same house. This is because they will have different risk experience for the area. Some insurers can purposely raise their prices to price themselves out of the market because they have had a bad experience in a particular area. When the subsidence crisis hit insurance companies, the Royal was particularly badly hit so it immediately doubled its rates and priced itself out of the market. It was easier to find someone cheaper.

There are a number of ways to reduce your premiums.

- If you are over 50 you can often get discounts: make sure to ask for them.

- You can also increase the excess you pay. This is the amount you pay yourself on any claim you make. Most policies have an excess of £50; if you increase this to £100 it qualifies you for a 5% discount. If you increase your excess to £1,000 you could halve your insurance bill. Most claims are, however, for £1,000 or less.

- You can decrease your premiums by having better security such as alarms or locks fitted.

- There are also discounts if you are in a Neighbourhood Watch scheme.

My own personal experience shows how much you can save. My household insurance was £303.37 a year. I saw an advert for household insurance for pharmacists (I am a self-employed pharmacist as well as a writer) so I rang out of curiosity. I was convinced that I had got a good price at the time already for my house insurance. They quoted me £163.49 per year and a free year every sixth year if I didn't make a claim. That one phone call will save me over £4,200 over 25 years.

You could decide not to have any contents insurance to reduce the cost of your insurance or you could have no buildings or contents insurance at all. Most mortgage lenders will insist on buildings insurance and I would recommend it. The table in Figure 15 shows how insurance quotes can vary. The quotes are for buildings and contents insurance for a £90,000 house with approximately £30,000 worth of contents in Telford Shropshire.

You can find a large list of home insurance companies in the *Yellow Pages*. There are also **Internet sites** which can help you save money on your home insurance:

- Screentrade   www.screentrade.com

- Find   www.find.co.uk/insurance

- Direct Line   www.directline.com

- Prudential   www.pru.co.uk

- Lloyds Bank   www.lloydstsb.com/insurance

- Norwich Union   www.norwich-union.co.uk

- AA   www.aa.com

- Churchill   www.churchill.com

- Abbey National   www.abbeynational.co.uk

Screentrade and Find will help you search for a variety of quotes to help you reduce your premiums.

Prudential	0800 300300	£303.37
Lloyds Bank	0800 834646	£228.65
Norwich Union	0800 888222	£169.31
AA	0800 444777	£276.90
Ecclesiastical	01952 224030*	£223.60
Gan	01952 224030*	£180.81
Churchill	0800 200345	£248.85
Abbey National	0800 670660	£272.14
Dial Direct	0800 0563921	£170.24
Pharmacy Mutual	0800 216118	£163.49

*via an insurance broker

Fig. 15. Quotes for buildings and contents insurance.

Checklist

Concentrate on the following points to ensure you save as much money as possible on your home insurance:

- Use telebrokers to reduce your premiums.
- Use the Internet brokers.
- Phone as many insurance companies as possible.
- Make sure you are getting the maximum discounts available to you for security measures or if you are over 50.
- Consider having a higher excess.
- Consider not having contents insurance.
- Make sure you are not overinsured or underinsured.
- Get new quotes each year when your policy is due for renewal from at least three companies.

HOME ENERGY COSTS

You may be wondering why there is a section on energy conservation in this book. The reason is that by conserving energy you will save yourself money each year. If you then use the money you save to help pay off your mortgage you will pay it off more quickly and save even more money.

It is possible to save several hundred pounds a year on household energy bills. I will also show you how the return you get from energy conservation is much better than investing your money in banks or building societies. Many energy conservation ideas cost nothing to implement and many others cost very little. So let's look at all the ideas listed in Figure 16. You can get a return of more than 30% on your money.

A three-year payback corresponds to an interest rate of 26%, four years to 19%, five years to 15%, nine years to 8% and eighteen years to 4%. Therefore if you look in the table for the time it takes for the costs to be recovered for various energy efficiency measures, you can see saving energy can be a better investment than leaving your money in banks or building societies.

In the example below, for cavity wall insulation you are getting a 19% return on your money compared to 5% return in a bank or building society. There are also many energy-saving measures that you can start without any money or very cheaply.

There are lots of good investments such as buying energy efficient appliances, e.g. refrigerators and freezers. A more efficient model may cost an extra £20 to £50 but it will save you £10 to £20 a year for at least 15 years. If your current appliances are over 10 years old, Figure 17 shows you the amounts you could save on your electricity bills each year.

The European Energy label has been designed to show the energy efficiency of appliances. 'A' rated appliances are the most efficient and 'G' are the most inefficient. Many old appliances will be very inefficient.

As you can see, you can save a lot of money by saving energy but you don't necessarily have to spend a lot of money to save on energy costs. Here are some low-cost measures and no-cost measures.

Low-cost measures

- Buy energy efficient light bulbs.
- Insulate your hot water tank.
- Insulate your hot water pipes.
- Use a shower instead of a bath.
- Fix dripping hot water taps.
- Draught proof exterior doors.

Energy-saving measure	Cost	Annual savings on fuel bills	Costs recovered
100mm top-up loft insulation	£75 (DIY) £200 (installer)	£35–£45	1–2 years (DIY) 4–5 years (installer)
150mm top-up loft insulation	£110 (DIY) £230 (installer)	£40–£50	2–3 years (DIY) 5–6 years (installer)
Fitting a jacket to your hot water tank	£10 (DIY) £30 (installer)	Up to £20	1 year (DIY) 2 years (installer)
Insulating hot water pipes	£10 (DIY)	Up to £5	2 years (DIY)
Cavity wall insulation	£450 (installer)	£75–£150	4 years
Internal wall insulation	£650 (installer)	£75–£100	6–7 years
External wall insulation	£1,500 (installer)	£85–£120	12–13 years
Draughtproofing	£50 (DIY) £150 (installer)	£15–£25	2 years (DIY) 6 years (installer)
Under-floor insulation	£75 (DIY)	£15–£30	2–3 years
Low energy lights	£5	£10	6 months
Partial central heating controls	£150–£300	£45–£70	3–7 years
Full central heating controls	£300–£450	£55–£85	5–8 years
Standard double glazing	£170 (installer)	£25–£30	5–6 years
Low-emissivity glazing	£275 (installer)	£30–£40	7–8 years
Secondary glazing	£200 (DIY)	£25–£30	6–7 years

Fig. 16. Energy-saving ideas.

Appliance	Energy rating	Average savings per year*
Fridge freezer	A B	£45 £40
Upright/chest freezer	A B	£35 £30
Fridge	A B	£25 £20
Washing machine	A	£15

*All the information is based on replacing an average (G energy rated) model currently in use with a similar size model and an electricity cost of 7p/kWh.

Fig. 17. Energy-saving appliances.

- Draught proof letterboxes and keyholes.
- Draught proof floorboards and skirting.
- Draught proof windows.

No-cost measures

- Turn your heating down by 1 degree C – this can save up to 10% on your heating bills.
- Set your hot water tank to about 60 degrees C/140 degrees F.
- Close your curtains as soon as it is dark.
- Turn off your lights.
- Do not leave electrical appliances on standby.
- Avoid putting hot food in a fridge.
- Put full loads in your washing machine or dryer.
- Don't overfill your kettle.

There are a number of energy advice centres throughout the country. They will offer you free advice on saving energy in your home. You can ring them up on the freephone number and they will send you out an energy survey for your home. You need to fill this in and send it back to them. They will then send you back all the recommendations to save you money on the energy costs in your home. The results will show you exactly how much you can save. In the case of my house they showed me how I could save £82 a year. They will also send you information leaflets on saving energy. It is all free and I would recommend that everyone gives them a call. They can even advise you on getting grants to have work done on your home to save energy.

Save Energy   0345 277200   www.saveenergy.co.uk

LIFE INSURANCE COSTS

Most people when they arrange a mortgage will arrange life insurance at the same time. Most lenders will insist that you have life insurance when you take out the mortgage. You may not have given a thought to the cost of life insurance which is a mistake. You could save thousands of pounds on the cost of life insurance by taking a small amount of time to search for the cheapest life insurance. There are a variety of life insurance products and it is important to have an understanding about them to save you money.

Term insurance

Term insurance is the most commonly used life insurance with mortgages, providing a specified level of cover for a certain period. It tends to be a cheap form of life insurance. This is partly due to the life insurance company being able to accurately work out the likelihood of having to pay out within a fixed term. Premiums are also lower because term insurance is not structured to pay out large commissions.

Premiums can vary enormously between identical term insurance policies. This is for a variety of reasons. Some companies may actually try to price themselves out of the market at times. This may be because they have had to pay out large claims and they now want to concentrate on other areas of business. Other companies can reduce their prices to try and attract more business.

There are six main types of term insurance: basic level term, increasing term, decreasing term, convertible term, family income benefit and pension term. **Critical illness insurance** is a more recent addition that is becoming more popular. This covers people against specific illnesses such as cancer and heart disease.

- **Basic level term** provides the same level of term insurance for a specified period of time. Therefore if you take out basic level term insurance of £40,000 for 20 years you will be covered for £40,000 for 20 years.

- **Increasing term** provides increasing levels of life insurance until the specified period is finished.

- **Decreasing term** provides decreasing levels of life insurance until the specified period is finished. Decreasing term is particularly useful with repayment mortgages where the amount you owe on the mortgage is gradually decreasing over the years. Decreasing term insurance can be a very cheap form of life insurance.

- **Convertible term** is term insurance that can be converted at any time to a **whole of life** policy (see below). A whole of life policy provides you with life cover for the whole of your life providing that you continue to pay your premiums. Whole of life insurance is usually more expensive than term insurance.

- **Family income benefit** provides your family with a monthly income if you die.

- **Pension term** insurance is the same as basic level term but you get tax relief on the cost of the life insurance within the pension. This can make pension term insurance a cheap form of life insurance.

There are some important points to note about term insurance.

- You can take out term insurance on a single or joint life basis.

- The term can be from 1 to 40 years upwards. The insurance company will pay out the agreed insurance sum assured if the insured person dies within the specified term. If the insured person outlives the term of the policy the contract lapses and the policyholder gets nothing. Also if the policy is cancelled before the end of the term the policyholder will get nothing back.

- The price of term insurance can be affected by your health, lifestyle, age, sex and occupation. If your health is poor you may be charged more for term insurance. Smokers tend to be charged more for life insurance owing to their greater likelihood of illness. If your occupation is more dangerous such as a racing driver you may be charged more for life insurance or if you have dangerous pastimes such as skydiving. In some cases you may even be declined life insurance.

We will look at ways to reduce your cost of life insurance later.

Endowments

Low cost mortgage endowments automatically have life insurance included in them. You will set the value of the life insurance when you initially take the policy out. Some endowment providers will allow you to alter the amount of life insurance within the policy. In most cases, however, the sum assured will remain the same throughout the policy. An endowment will therefore provide death benefit until the end of the policy term.

Whole of life policy

A whole of life policy differs from term insurance in that providing you keep paying the premiums of the policy you will be covered with life insurance. Therefore there is no specified period for the policy to run. Therefore your life insurance cover will not expire at some date in the future as in the case of a term insurance policy. The drawback of this type of life insurance is that it is more expensive than term insurance.

Reducing the cost of life insurance

It is important to speak to an IFA about life insurance. They will probably be able to save you a lot of money compared to the high street banks and building societies. It is important first of all to discuss the type of life insurance that you need. The cheapest types of life insurance are decreasing term insurance and pension term insurance. Although they may not be suitable for your situation, it is worth asking about them. A very important point to make here is that many people are woefully under-insured. It is also very important to try and make adequate life insurance provisions for your dependants. An IFA can give you a guide as to what level of life insurance you should be aiming at. We will now look at some life insurance quotes to see how much an IFA could save you.

Here are quotes for **£100,000 of term insurance for a male non-smoker aged 30 over 25 years:**

Company	Monthly premium	Saving per month	Saving over 25 years
Legal and General	£8.70	£0.00	£0.00
Friends Provident	£9.90	£1.20	£360.00
Swiss Life	£10.57	£1.87	£561.00
Scottish Provident	£10.81	£2.11	£633.00
Allied Dunbar	£15.00	£6.30	£1,890.00
Canada Life	£15.50	£6.80	£2,040.00

As you can see from these quotes, you could save up to £2,040 by choosing a cheaper life insurer. You could save even more than this if you are looking at insuring yourselves for more over a longer period of time. If you are a smoker your premiums will be higher with most companies and the differences in price can be larger.

Overleaf are quotes for **£100,000 of term insurance for a male smoker aged 30 over 25 years.**

In the case of a smoker you would save up to £3,060. You can also reduce the cost of your life insurance by choosing the best type of life insurance policy to suit your needs. Decreasing term insurance is cheaper than basic term insurance and may suit your situation.

Company	Monthly premium	Saving per month	Saving over 25 years
Legal and General	£15.40	£0.00	£0.00
Friends Provident	£15.91	£0.51	£153.00
Swiss Life	£16.66	£1.26	£378.00
Scottish Provident	£17.11	£1.71	£513.00
Canada Life	£20.80	£5.40	£1,620.00
Allied Dunbar	£25.60	£10.20	£3,060.00

Now we look at quotes for **£100,000 of insurance for a 30-year-old male over 25 years**.

As you can see you could save up to £1,350 in this example by choosing decreasing term insurance. It is very important, however, to make sure you have the correct type of life cover for your situation and make sure that you

Company	Basic insurance	Decreasing term insurance	Saving per month	Saving over 25 years
Legal and General	£8.70	£7.00	£1.70	£510.00
Scottish Provident	£10.81	£8.64	£2.17	£651.00
Standard Life	£10.59	£8.86	£1.73	£519.00
Canada Life	£15.50	£11.00	£4.50	£1,350.00

are not under-insured. Take the advice of the IFA on the type of life cover you need but ask why he is recommending that type of life cover and if there is a cheaper alternative. We will now look at a typical life insurance quote which will give you information about the life insurance costs.

Male, age next birthday 32, non smoker, single

1. Guaranteed life cover £50,000. Policy term 20 years.

2. Guaranteed monthly premium £6.40.

What benefits does the plan provide?

3. Guaranteed life cover £50,000.

The life cover will be payable should you die within the term of the policy. You may increase the level of cover without further medical information, on your marriage, birth of your child or when you move or improve your home, subject to certain conditions.

4. Warning:
   This contract has no cash-in value at any time.

   Your premiums pay for the cost of life cover, commission, expenses, charges and other adjustments.

How much will the advice cost?

5. For arranging the contract, company will pay commission to your financial adviser worth £111.70 immediately and then from month 49, £0.16 each month until the end of the plan.
   The amount will depend on the size of your premium and the length of the term of the contract. It will be paid for out of the premiums.

Notes:

1. This gives the details that the quote is based upon. It is important to check that these details are correct and the quote is for the correct amount of life cover and type of policy that you require.

2. This details the cost of the policy. This is the most important part. You are looking for the cheapest policy that suits you. The cheapest policy may be reviewable after a period of time when the company may raise· the cost of the life insurance. Make sure you check these details and make sure you are happy with them. You will need to look at two or three quotes to determine which is the cheapest and which suits you the best. It is important to check if the premiums remain the same throughout the policy or are to be revised after a certain period of time.

3. This gives you details of the benefits of the policy. You need to check that you are covered for the correct amount of life cover. Then you need to check what other benefits are available under the policy. This policy enables you to increase your life cover in the event of marriage, children and moving house without medical information under certain conditions. This may well be useful to certain people particularly if they have poor health. Life insurance policies can have a very wide range of extra benefits added to them such as terminal illness benefit, and waiver of premium benefit to mention a few. You need to talk carefully to the

financial adviser about what protection you want and then look for the right benefits. In general the more benefits you have the more expensive the policy will be.

4. This tells you that this policy has no cash-in value. Therefore if you stop this policy early or at maturity you will get no cash back. Certain policies such as endowment or a whole of life policy may well have cash-in values. This also tells you what your premiums go towards paying.

5. This tells you how much the financial adviser will earn from the commission of the policy. Remember that if you are paying the financial adviser on a fee basis you should expect all of this back. If you are paying on a commission basis you may still be able to negotiate some of this back. The typical commission for a life insurance policy is all of the first year's premiums plus a monthly commission of 2.5% after 4 years. If we use the case of a 35-year-old non-smoker taking out a £100,000 term insurance policy over 20 years, one company would charge £15.94 a month, £304.92 would be paid out in commission initially then 39p a month after month 49 of the contract.

A salesman could, however, earn more commission by offering a less competitive product. Another company, for example, would pay out £379 initially but their premiums are about 25% higher than the first company.

Reducing the cost of life insurance yourself

You can personally have an effect on the cost of your life insurance. Life insurance costs are based on your health, age and sex. Probably about 90% of people will have life insurance based on standard rates. There are groups of people who are charged more for their life insurance. **Smokers** are the main group of people who are charged more for their life insurance.There are some companies that treat cigar or pipe smokers as non-smokers. Therefore you could give up smoking to save on life insurance costs and perhaps improve your health.

People who are engaged in **hazardous occupations or pastimes** will often find that they will be charged more for life insurance. Therefore a parachute instructor may well have to pay more than the office worker for life insurance or be declined. If you take part in dangerous pastimes this can affect your premiums. Sports such as motor racing, mountaineering and parachuting can raise the premiums of your life insurance.

Life insurance premiums are also based on your **general level of health**. You will be asked questions about your weight, height, drinking habits, medical condition and a range of other questions to try and determine your health. Most people will be offered life insurance premiums at a standard rate but a small minority of people may be charged higher rates. This may be because they are very overweight, or the insurance company thinks of them as a high risk. There are one or two companies that offer lower life insurance quotes to practitioners of transcendental meditation because it has been shown to reduce their chance of illness. All of these ideas involve changes in lifestyle which many people will not want to make. As I have already said, most people will be offered standard rates; if you are asked to pay higher rates then approach a number of different companies.

To summarise, here are a few ways of possibly reducing life insurance premiums:

● Use an IFA to arrange your life insurance.

● Stop smoking.

● Change to a less hazardous job.

● Stop hazardous sports.

● Improve your health.

● Reduce your weight to normal.

● Drink less alcohol.

● Learn transendental meditation.

If you stop smoking this will have the greatest effect on premiums. The other factors may not affect premiums unless you are in poor health. If you take out life insurance and your health improves or job becomes less hazardous you can approach your existing company to see if they will reduce your life insurance premiums. You can also get some new quotes from other life insurance companies to see if you may be able to reduce the cost of your life insurance.

Do you need life insurance at all?

You may not need any life insurance at all and you could save yourself all your life insurance costs. If you have no dependants and no one that you would like to leave your house to, there is an argument to say that you don't need any life insurance.

It is possible to start your mortgage off on a repayment or interest only basis without any life insurance. Then if you need life insurance at a later date you can arrange this. Most people will take out life insurance when they start their mortgage but it may be unnecessary. A lot of mortgage lenders will try and make you take out a life insurance policy for two reasons. Firstly they may well be able to earn commission from the policy. Secondly if you die the policy will pay out and the mortgage lender will get their money quickly. If you die without a life insurance policy to pay off the mortgage the lender will have to sell the house which will take more time and effort for them. Therefore mortgage lenders tend to push life insurance products for their benefit. If your lender insists on their insurance product but you have no need for it you may be better off looking for another lender who does not insist on life insurance.

It is important to check whether or not you may have any life insurance benefits from your employer. Many employees get death-in-service benefits from their employer that may be sufficient to cover your mortgage. This would make any extra life insurance unnecessary.

You must remember, though, that if you have any dependants, you do need life insurance. Many people are woefully under-insured. Don't make this mistake – make sure you are adequately insured if you have dependants.

Summary of life insurance

The two most important aspects of life insurance are making sure that you have got the correct life insurance and that you are paying the cheapest possible price for it. You need to discuss in detail with an IFA to decide which type of life insurance you need. There are a vast array of possible benefits to suit every client. Do not assume that the high street banks and building societies will offer you the best rates, in most cases they won't.

An IFA will be able to look through all the companies in the marketplace and find out which company is the cheapest. Remember, you could save thousands of pounds by getting a cheaper policy. Review your policy every few years or so because the cost of life insurance varies as companies try to gain a larger share of the market. I took out a whole of life policy for my wife and myself for £150,000 which cost £30 a month. This ran for several years until I just looked at it again out of interest and found another company that offered £150,000 for £20 a month. That one phone call will save me £3,600 over thirty years.

SOURCES OF INFORMATION

The first source of information is an IFA. They will have computers that can check all the life insurance quotes to find the most competitive. They will also be able to get the brochures from the companies to check what benefits the companies can offer you and which will suit you best. Here are two IFAs I have used:

Bryan Davies and Company Ltd, 44 High Street, Bridgnorth, Shropshire, WV16 4DX. Tel: 01746 764446.

Rob Hodson. Tel: 07881 823760.

Another source of reference is *Money Management Magazine* which has a list of term insurance rates each month. This can be obtained from good newsagents.

Moneyfacts can also provide information on level term insurance if you have a fax machine. You just pick up the handset of your fax machine and dial the number then press the start button on your fax machine when prompted. The telephone number is 0336 400 853. Calls will cost a maximum of 50p/minute. Moneyfacts can be telephoned on 01692 500 765 for more information. The level term insurance rates are updated monthly on their service.

CHECKLIST

- Check with an IFA what levels and which types of life insurance you need.

- Ask why the IFA has recommended this policy and if there is a cheaper alternative.

- Look at the life insurance quote carefully and ask questions until you understand it.

- What is the cost of the policy? Will this remain the same throughout the life of the policy or can it alter?

- What are the benefits of the policy? Do these benefits match what you need?

- Are there any cheaper quotes? Is there any way of reducing the cost with the same benefits?

- If you are paying a fee-based adviser ask for the commission back. If you have a commission-based adviser ask for some of the commission back.

9

Remortgaging

Remortgaging can save you a lot of money on your mortgage costs, but there are often costs involved which have to be taken into account. It is best to use an IFA (Independent Financial Adviser) or a mortgage broker because they will have access to thousands of mortgages. They will also be able to take you easily through the following steps.

DECIDE WHAT YOU WANT FROM A REMORTGAGE

This is the first step when considering a remortgage. It is important to know what you are looking for in a remortgage. You can get discounts off the standard rate, lower variable rates and cash back incentives. Lenders can offer you a discounted rate for an initial period on remortgages which can reduce your mortgage payments substantially. You have to be careful what the interest rate reverts to after the discounted period and if there are any extended penalty periods.

Some direct lenders can also offer lower standard rates than many high street lenders. When remortgaging for a lower standard rate, you have to look particularly at the cost of remortgaging, because the savings have to outweigh the costs for it to be worthwhile.

Lenders can also offer cash bank incentives for remortgaging. You have to look closely at what the mortgage rate will be when you have remortgaged and if there are any redemption fees during the initial period of the mortgage.

You need to ask yourself the following questions:

- Do you want a cheaper monthly mortgage?

- Do you need a much cheaper mortgage for a short period of time, which then reverts to a similar mortgage payment to your current mortgage?

- Do you want a cash lump sum?

- Do you want to fix or cap your mortgage?

- Do you need to raise extra cash for house extensions or for other purposes?

- Are you willing to accept redemption penalties beyond the initial incentive period?

When you know the answers to these questions you can ask the IFA or mortgage broker to look at what is available. It is important to spend time finding a good mortgage adviser because they can save you thousands of pounds.

CHECK IF THERE WILL BE ANY REDEMPTION FEES ON YOUR CURRENT MORTGAGE

Many mortgages have redemption fees if you change your mortgage. This is particularly the case with fixed rate, capped, discount or cash back mortgages. Whenever the mortgage lender offers you a special rate they will usually charge redemption fees if you change your mortgage within a specified period of time. They can often charge you three to six months worth of interest which is a lot of money. If you are looking at remortgaging and your current mortgage has redemption penalties it is often better to wait until there are no longer any redemption penalties.

Some lenders will allow you to change mortgage with themselves without any penalties. This may be useful if the lender has a new mortgage that suits you. You can move your mortgage even if you have to pay redemption fees but the new mortgage would have to be very good indeed to make it worthwhile. Therefore check the redemption fees before you move your mortgage.

WORK OUT THE COST OF YOUR CURRENT MORTGAGE

You need to know the details about your current mortgage. These include:

- your current mortgage interest rate

- exactly how much your current mortgage costs you

- whether you are getting any discounts or special mortgage rates at the moment

- how much your mortgage will cost you over the whole term of the mortgage

- the loan to value (LTV) ratio.

You can then use all the information to help compare your mortgage against other mortgages that you are interested in. It is very important to look at the total cost of the mortgage over the whole term. It is no use saving a small amount of money in the short term if it will cost you a lot more money in the long term. Use your information about your own mortgage to look for a better deal from other lenders.

FIND OUT THE COSTS OF REMORTGAGING

The usual costs of remortgaging can involve the following fees:

- solicitors' fees
- mortgage arrangement fees
- valuation fees
- Mortgage Indemnity Guarantee premiums
- redemption fees.

You need to know what costs are involved before you remortgage. The solicitors' fees and valuation fees can add up to several hundred pounds and they are usually linked to the value of your house. Mortgage arrangement fees can often be avoided by choosing a lender that doesn't charge them. You may have to pay a Mortgage Indemnity Guarantee premium (MIG) which could be very expensive, but if you are borrowing less than 75% of the value of the property you will not pay MIG. Some lenders do not charge MIG and other lenders only charge MIG above 90% LTV. Redemption penalties tend to be payable on fixed, capped or special mortgages. These can often be avoided if you wait until the redemption period has finished. These costs need to be taken into account when looking to save money.

This is why it is always worth asking your current lender to see if they will match a remortgage offer. If your current lender will match a remortgage offer you will probably be better staying with them, owing to the costs and inconveniences involved in remortgaging. There are a growing number of lenders who are reducing the cost of remortgaging by offering free valuations, free legal fees and making it easier to remortgage.

WORK OUT IF REMORTGAGING WILL SAVE YOU MONEY

When you have all the information you need about your current mortgage and the remortgage you are interested in, you need to sit down and work out if the remortgage will save you money and how much. You need to list out all the costs involved in remortgaging. The current costs of your current mortgage should be listed. Then list the monthly costs of the mortgage payments for your current mortgage and remortgage. You need to be saving some money to make the inconvenience of the remortgaging worthwhile. Remortgaging will involve some time and effort on your part and can be stressful but it can save you money. When you are sure that remortgaging will save you money and your current lender will not match your remortgage offer then proceed with the remortgaging.

ASK YOUR CURRENT LENDER TO MATCH OR BETTER THE REMORTGAGE OFFER

Mortgage lending is very competitive and mortgage lenders are very keen to keep their clients, particularly if you have been a good client. Therefore when you have got a remortgage offer that suits you go back to your current lender with all the details and see if they can match or better the offer. Initially suggest to them that they need to better the offer for you to stay with them. If they do, even more money will be saved. Even if they are only prepared to match the offer it will probably be cheaper and less stressful to stay with your current lender.

Most people do not realise that you can negotiate with your current lender like this but it happens every day. It is best to go armed with information on what other lenders will offer you to put your current lender under pressure. Remember it is just asking for a cheaper rate that could save you a lot of money.

PROCEED WITH THE REMORTGAGE

Once you have gone back to your current lender and they will not match or improve on your remortgage offer it is time to proceed, if you are happy with the advantages of the remortgage. Remortgaging will usually take about 8 weeks, but it can take as little as 4 weeks. The solicitors will have to carry their work out and the valuers will have to value your property. Remortgaging can be worthwhile as we will now show.

Remortgage over 25 years assuming current mortgage is running for 25 years on a repayment basis:

Mortgage	Interest rate APR	Monthly cost	Total cost
£80,000	5.25%	£484.80	£145,440
£80,000	5.75%	£508.80	£152,640

Therefore the saving would be £7,200 over 25 years if you could reduce your interest rate by 0.5%. Obviously over a shorter period such as 10 to 15 years the savings would be less but they can still outweigh the costs of solicitors' fees, valuation fees and any other costs.

> While writing this book I looked at remortgaging my house. I had a mortgage of £80,000 on a £90,000 house. I had a fixed rate of 7.99% for 5 years that was coming to the end of its 5 years. I waited until the end of the fixed period when there would be no redemption penalties. I eventually decided to remortgage with a lender that offered a flexible mortgage. The interest rate was 5.6% fixed for 5 years. This saved me £140 a month on my mortgage payment. The remortgage was a fees-free transfer so there was no cost to me. The new mortgage was a flexible mortgage so that I could have the flexibility to overpay or borrow back the overpayments. The remortgage will save me £8,400 over 5 years. So you can see I saved a lot of money by remortgaging. You may be able to do the same.

These are two IFAs that I have used:

Bryan Davies, 44 High Street, Bridgnorth, Shropshire, WV16 4DX. Tel: 01746 764446.

Rob Hodson. Tel: 07881 823760.

Remortgage contacts
Charcol. Tel: 0800 718191 or www.charcolonline.co.uk (Charcol are one of the largest mortgage brokers in the country.)

Chase de Vere. Tel: 020 7930 7242 or www.cdvmortgage.co.uk (Chase de Vere are a large mortgage brokers.)

Mortgage answers. Tel: 0800 195 2485 or www.winterthur-life.co.uk (You can ring the phone number to find your local representative or visit the website.)

IFA promotion. Tel: 01179 711 177 or www.unbiased.co.uk (can give you details of three Independent Financial Advisers near where you live or work.)

CHECKLIST

● Contact an IFA or mortgage broker to discuss what you are looking for and to see what is available.

- Check all the details of your current mortgage:
  - The interest rate charged.
  - The monthly cost of your mortgage.
  - Are there any special discounts or rates that you have currently?
  - Are there any redemption fees that will be charged with your mortgage?
  - What will your mortgage cost you in total over the term of the mortgage?

- Make sure you know all the details of the remortgage offer:
  - The costs involved; for example, solicitors' fees, valuation fees, mortgaging arrangement fees and any Mortgage Indemnity Guarantee premium.
  - The interest rate charged.
  - The monthly cost of the remortgage.
  - Will there be any redemption charges with the new mortgage and will they extend beyond the incentive period?
  - What will the new mortgage cost you in total over the term of the mortgage?
  - The savings you can make with the remortgage.

- Go back to your current lender and ask if they will better or match your remortgage offer.

- Go ahead with the remortgage if you are happy with everything.

10

Halve the Cost of Buying
Your Home

The four golden rules for paying as little as possible for your house are:

1. Buy your house for as little as possible.

2. Borrow as little as possible using a mortgage.

3. Pay your mortgage off as quickly as possible.

4. Borrow money at the cheapest rate possible.

This chapter is designed to help summarise the whole book and give you reminders of ways to reduce the cost of your house. By using one or two ideas you will save yourself thousands of pounds. By using as many ideas as possible you will save yourself tens of thousands of pounds.

BUY YOUR HOUSE FOR AS LITTLE AS POSSIBLE

- Consider buying your house at an auction.

- Consider building your own home.

- Buy your house in the normal manner by negotiating the price down.

- Remember that everything is negotiable – if the vendor will not move on price he may include extras.

- Buy a repossession house.

- Reduce your buying costs.

Remember that the initial cost of your house is the purchase price plus all the other extras such as solicitors' fees, mortgage guarantee premiums, etc. and all the other expenses. People also often forget their own time and effort. Everything has to be paid out of your own pocket. Spend time looking and negotiating and you can save thousands of pounds.

Building your own house can save on average about 30% of the final value of the house. Repossessions can often be 10% to 30% cheaper than their market value. You have to be more careful at auctions because you can overbid, but bargains can be had. Then you can always negotiate a normal sale with a vendor and save yourself thousands of pounds.

Most people just find a house then quickly arrange the mortgage without much thought as to how they could save on the cost of the house. You need to look at how much the house you want should be worth and then look at ways of buying it more cheaply.

Let us take an example to show you what differences you can make. If we look at buying a £70,000 house the table in Figure 18 could show you what you could save by reducing the purchase price of the house by negotiating or making a good purchase. Remember every thousand pounds saved at 5.75% will save you £1,908. If the interest rate is higher you will be saving more.

A saving of £10,000 on a £70,000 house is a saving of 14% on the purchase price. You can often save more than this if you plan your purchase carefully.

BORROW AS LITTLE AS POSSIBLE USING A MORTGAGE

This is the most important factor of the total cost of your house. The less you can borrow to pay for your house the less expensive it will be. You will be charged interest on every pound you borrow. The cheapest possible way to pay for a house is to save the money up and pay for the whole house without borrowing anything. Too few people do this. The few that do will save tens of thousands of pounds. Many people will not be able to do this but it is still important to try and save as much towards your house as possible.

Let's look at some examples. In these examples we have quoted the figures on an 5.75% repayment mortgage. The total cost is the cost of the mortgage over 25 years and the deposit added together to show you the total cost over 25 years.

Repayment mortgage amount	Cost per month over 25 years at 5.75%	Total cost over 25 years
£70,000	£445.20	£133,560
£65,000	£413.40	£124,020
£61,000	£387.96	£116,388
£60,000	£381.60	£114,480

Fig. 18. Saving by reducing the purchase price.

As you can see from the table in Figure 19, if you pay cash for a £60,000 house it will cost about half price compared to someone who pays for it all over 25 years at 5.75%. Therefore the most important point here is to try and borrow as little as possible. Try and save as big a deposit towards your house as possible.

Cost of the house	Deposit paid	Mortgage amount	Cost per month	Total cost
£60,000	£0	£60,000	£381.60	£114,480
£60,000	£10,000	£50,000	£318.00	£105,400
£60,000	£20,000	£40,000	£254.40	£96,320
£60,000	£30,000	£30,000	£190.80	£87,240
£60,000	£40,000	£20,000	£127.20	£78,160
£60,000	£50,000	£10,000	£63.60	£69,080
£60,000	£60,000	£0	£0	£60,000

Fig. 19. Borrowing as little as possible.

PAY YOUR MORTGAGE OFF AS QUICKLY AS POSSIBLE

The longer that you borrow money using a mortgage the more it will cost you. Therefore try and reduce the mortgage term as much as possible. Let's look at some examples. Figure 20 shows a table for a repayment mortgage at 5.75%.

As you can see from these examples, if you had a 30-year repayment mortgage for £60,000 at 5.75% it would cost you £127,224, whereas over 10 years it would cost you £80,568 which is a big saving. The examples show very clearly how reducing the term of your mortgage can save you money. Now you may well be saying to me, I can't afford to pay more on my mortgage repayment. This is quite a reasonable thing to say. However, you need to realise that any small increases you can make in your mortgage payment can make a large difference over the longer term.

If we look at the 30-year and 25-year quote you will see that the 25-year term will cost you £28.20 more a month but it will save you £12,744. What you can do is gradually increase your mortgage payment by £5.00 or £10.00 each year when you get a pay rise.

Another way of shortening your mortgage term is, when your mortgage rate goes down and your monthly payment goes down, you can ask for your

Mortgage amount	Term of mortgage	Monthly cost	Cost over whole term of mortgage
£60,000	30 years	£353.40	£127,224
£60,000	25 years	£381.60	£114,480
£60,000	20 years	£427.20	£102,528
£60,000	15 years	£506.40	£91,152
£60,000	10 years	£671.40	£80,568
£60,000	Cash paid	£0	£60,000

Fig. 20. Reducing the term of your mortgage.

payment to be maintained at its original level and for the capital of the mortgage to be paid off. If your mortgage payment is £350 a month and the interest rate reduces so that your mortgage payment goes down to £340 a month, you can ask the mortgage company to maintain your payment at £350 a month. You must, however, instruct them to use the £10 a month to reduce your capital on your mortgage because they will not automatically do this. This overpayment of £10 a month will reduce the term of your mortgage and save you money.

Anything you can do to reduce your mortgage term such as paying lump sums off your mortgage, increasing your monthly mortgage payment or increasing a savings plan to pay off your mortgage more quickly will save you money. The flexible mortgages now available allow you to make over-payments to pay your mortgage off more quickly. You also still have access to these overpayments at any time.

BORROW MONEY AT THE CHEAPEST RATE POSSIBLE

The rate at which you borrow money for a mortgage determines how much interest you will pay and how much it will cost you. It is important to try and arrange the cheapest lending you can get over the whole term of the mortgage. Let's look at some examples of a 25-year repayment mortgage.

As you can see from the table in Figure 21, a 0.25% rise in interest rates can mean an increase of £2,880 on the cost of a mortgage over 25 years. A 1% rise could mean an increased cost of £10,980 over 25 years. It is very important when looking at lenders to look at what rate you will be paying in the long term and not concentrate on the special offer they may have for 2 or 3 years.

Mortgage amount	Interest rate	Monthly cost	Total cost
£60,000	5%	£354.60	£106,380
£60,000	5.25%	£363.60	£109,080
£60,000	5.50%	£372.60	£111,780
£60,000	5.75%	£381.60	£114,480
£60,000	6%	£391.20	£117,360

Fig. 21. Borrowing money at the cheapest rate.

You will often be able to reduce your regular borrowing by 0.25% to 0.5% by choosing a more competitive lender. The direct lenders as discussed in earlier chapters can often offer variable rates 0.5% lower than the high street lenders owing to their lower overheads and because they charge interest daily.

You may well be able to negotiate a lower rate with your own lender by suggesting to them that you will move your mortgage to another lender unless they reduce your mortgage rate. If they will not reduce your rate you can then look at remortgaging to reduce your interest rate. Remember that interest rates are not written in stone and you can negotiate lower rates. The mortgage marketplace is very competitive and large lenders are very keen to hold on to business.

The following two examples can show you how much this book could save you when you put the ideas in this book into practice.

Example 1

Mr Jakes buys a £90,000 house with a £10,000 deposit and then pays for his house over 25 years at 6% with his bank or building society. He arranges a repayment mortgage which costs him £521.60 a month. He arranges his buildings and contents insurance and life assurance through the bank and building society and he doesn't try to save any money on his heating bills.

Example 2

Mr Sharp builds his own house or buys it at an auction to save 30% on the price of the house. He therefore doesn't have to pay Stamp Duty or a mortgage indemnity guarantee premium. He negotiates a reduction in the valuation fees and the mortgage arrangement fees. He phones telebrokers to reduce his house insurance and an IFA for life insurance. He arranges the house removal himself. Then he arranges a mortgage at a slightly reduced rate of 5.25% and he keeps the mortgage term short to 15 years. The 15-year repayment mortgage costs him £456.96 a month. He also insulates his home well and reduces his heating costs.

If you look at the table in Figure 22 the largest cost is the mortgage cost. Therefore your biggest savings can be made by concentrating on:

1. **borrowing as little as possible using a mortgage**
2. **paying your mortgage off as quickly as possible**
3. **borrowing money at the cheapest rate possible.**

Many of the other savings can be achieved just by making a few phone calls. By ringing an IFA you can save on life insurance and mortgage costs. If you phone the Energy Efficiency line and carry out their advice you will save money. By phoning telebrokers you could save £4,625 on buildings and contents insurance. If you spend just a little time you can save thousands of pounds. How long would it take you to save up £5,000 in a bank? You could save yourself that much with one phone call. As we can see using all the ideas from this book you can pay half price or less for your house.

While writing and researching this book I have used the information in this book to save myself money. I changed my mortgage and saved £140 a month on my mortgage payment. I changed my life insurance and saved £10 a month. I also negotiated to have some of the commission to be paid back to me on the new policy. I have improved the energy savings in our home and saved £100 a year. I changed my home insurance and saved £139.88 a year. I also got rid of an insurance policy for my flat that I didn't need and saved £35 a year. In total I have saved myself £2,074.88 a year. This could mean a saving of £51,872 over 25 years.

Expense	Initial cost Example 1 Mr Jakes	Cost over 25 years	Initial cost Example 2 Mr Sharp	Cost over 25 years
House value	£90,000		£90,000	
Price paid	£90,000		£56,000	
Deposit paid	£10,000	£10,000	£0	£0
Stamp Duty	£800	£800	£0	£0
MIG	£1,000	£1,000	£0	£0
Valuation fee	£165	£165	£140	£140
Home insurance	£370	£9,250	£185	£4,625
Arrangement fees	£250	£250	£0	£0
Removal costs	£400	£400	£50	£50
Home furnishings	£4,000	£4,000	£1,000	£1,000
Mortgage cost	£80,000	£156,480	£56,000	£82,252.80
Life insurance	£58.51	£17,553	£25.02	£7,507
Heating	£600	£15,000	£400	£10,000
Total		£214,898		£105,574.80
Saving		£0		£109,323.20
% saving		0%		50.9%

Fig. 22. Putting the ideas in this book into practice.

Tips and Ideas for Saving Money on the Cost of Your House

The following is a list of ideas of how you can save money on the total cost of your house. These ideas are listed in no particular order but they could save you a lot of money.

1. Build your own house.

2. Learn to negotiate to save yourself money.

3. Remember negotiating is just asking.

4. Go to house auctions.

5. Buy your house at an auction.

6. Negotiate a reduced price from the vendor.

7. Negotiate for extras such as carpets and curtains.

8. Look to reduce the purchase price to reduce Stamp Duty.

9. Look to reduce the mortgage indemnity guarantee premium (MIG) by paying a larger deposit or choosing a lender that does not charge it.

10. Reduce your solicitors' costs by negotiating.

11. Reduce your valuation fees by negotiating.

12. Buy a repossession property at reduced price.

13. Buy a run down property at a reduced price.

14. Move house yourself and save money.

15. Avoid mortgage arrangement fees.

16. Choose an IFA that offers you the choice of working on a fee basis or commission.

17. If the IFA works on a fee basis ask for any commission back for yourself.

18. If the IFA works on commission you can still negotiate for some of it back.

19. When looking at saving plans, good performance is an important factor to consider, and try to choose a strong company.

20. Look for good performance and low costs ideally in the case of a savings plan.

21. When moving house with a repayment mortgage take out a new repayment mortgage that is as short a term as you can afford.

22. Consider increasing your monthly mortgage payment to reduce the cost of your house.

23. Consider paying lump sums off your mortgage.

24. Consider increasing your mortgage payment each year as your wages increase.

25. When your mortgage rate reduces ask your lender to keep the payments the same to reduce the capital you owe.

26. Try to choose a lender that charges interest daily.

27. Consider direct lenders to save money on the standard variable rate.

28. Consider a flexible mortgage to make overpayments and have the facility to get these back.

29. Consider increasing your savings plan to reduce the mortgage term.

30. When moving with an interest only mortgage try and keep the mortgage term to the same length as you originally took out or even shorten it.

31. Try and keep a clean credit history and avoid CCJs or arrears.

32. Use an IFA to reduce your life insurance costs.

33. Use telebrokers to try to reduce the cost of your buildings and contents insurance.

34. Get a heat insulation survey done on your house and improve your home insulation.

35. Ask your current lender to reduce your current mortgage interest rate.

36. Look at remortgaging to reduce your mortgage costs if your current lender will not consider reducing their rates.

37. Consider decreasing term insurance to reduce your life insurance costs where appropriate.

38. Borrow as little as possible on your mortgage.

39. Pay your mortgage off as quickly as possible. You can use any unexpected cash lump sums, for example a lottery win.

40. Consider sharing to get yourself on the housing ladder.

41. Consider asking to have a larger excess on your building and contents insurance.

42. Consider paying your mortgage more frequently; for example, every 4 weeks, every fortnight or even weekly.

43. Try not to extend your mortgage term – it will cost you more money.

44. Mortgage rates have averaged between 11% to 12% over the long term – consider fixing your interest rates when mortgage rates are low.

45. Flexible mortgages can provide you with a cheaper source of funds than an unsecured loan for cars and holidays if you have built up a reserve.

46. Regularly review items such as life insurance, buildings and contents because the costs of these can be reduced by companies wanting more market share.

47. Consider just saving up for your house and not having a mortgage at all.

48. Keep looking at ways to reduce the cost of your house. Talk to IFAs and keep your eye on the financial pages in the papers.

49. Consider buying a smaller house.

50. Read this book several times completely and put the ideas into action!

I hope you save a lot of money! It is up to you now!

Useful Contacts and Further Information

AUCTIONEERS

Allsop & Co.	020 7437 6977	www.allsopp.co.uk
Athawes Son & Co.	020 8992 0056	
Hambro Countrywide	01245 344 133	
Halifax Property Services	01509 680 701	www.halifax.co.uk
Jones and Chapman	01253 612 000	www.wheretolive.co.uk
Roy Pugh	01772 883 399	www.pugh-company.co.uk
Winkworths	020 8649 7255	www.eigroup.co.uk

- An independent company called Faxwise will send you catalogues and details of all property auctions for three months at a cost of £100. For details Tel: 020 7720 5000.

- A company called P.D.S is a property brokerage dealing exclusively with repossessed properties, land and properties in need of refurbishment and renovation. For details Tel: 01494 444096.

- The *Estate Gazette* is a publication that you can buy from newsagents which contains details of auction houses, current prices and auctions. It is worth buying a copy.

BUILDING YOUR OWN HOME

Build It – this magazine covers all aspects of designing and building your own home. Available from newsagents.

Building your Own Home (300 pages) – deals with every aspect of building your own home. Tel: 01909 591652.

The Complete and Essential Guide to Building your Own Home by

Rosalind Renshaw (200 pages). Advice and information on all aspects of building a house. Tel: 020 7865 9042.

The Housebuilders Bible – covers all aspects of building a house, written by a self-builder. Tel: 01223 290230.

Insurance for self-building

DMS Services Ltd. Tel: 01909 591652.
Holbrook Insurance Brokers. Tel: 01483 505932.

Plots of land

Build It magazine – often lists plots of land for sale.
Landbank Services Ltd. Tel: 0118 962 6022.

Natural Plotfinder Database Tel: 0906 557 5400.

Websites

Home Builder (self-build information)   www.gold.net
Self Build and Design magazine   www.selfbuildanddesign.com

Homebuilding magazine   www.homebuilding.co.uk

FIXED PRICE CONVEYANCING

Central Legal and Conveyancing. Tel: 0808 1446343.

IFAs (INDEPENDENT FINANCIAL ADVISERS)

The following IFAs can advise you on all types of mortgages from negative equity to self-employed mortgages. They can also advise you on savings products.

Bryan Davies and Company Ltd, 44 High Street, Bridgnorth, Shropshire, WV16 4DX. Tel: 01746 764446. Tel: 01746 764446.

Rob Hodson. Tel: 07881 823760.

IFA promotion. Tel: 01179 711 177 or www.unbiased.co.uk can give you details of three Independent Financial Advisers near where you live or work.

MORTGAGES CONTACTS

Charcol. Tel: 0800 718191 or www.charcolonline.co.uk (Charcol are one of the largest mortgage brokers in the country.)

Chase de Vere. Tel: 020 7930 7242 or www.cdvmortgage.co.uk (Chase de Vere are a large mortgage brokers.)

Mortgage Answers. Tel: 0800 195 2485 or www.winterthur-life.co.uk (you can ring the phone number to find your local representative or visit the website.)

Mortgage lenders dealing with CCJs and arrears

Kensington Mortgage Company	0800 111020	www.kmc.co.uk
The Mortgage Business	08457 253253	www.t-m-b-co.uk

Mortgage lenders dealing with negative equity

The Mortgage Business	08457 253253	www.t-m-b-co.uk
Bristol & West	0845 3008000	www.bristol-west.co.uk
Bradford & Bingley	08457 852852	www.bradford-bingley.co.uk
Mortgage Express	0500 212854	www.mortgage-express.co.uk
Abbey National	0800 555100	www.abbeynational.co.uk
Woolwich	08459 757575	www.woolwich.co.uk
Halifax	0800 203049	www.halifax.co.uk
Cheltenham & Gloucester	0500 246810	www.cheltglos.co.uk
Bank of Scotland	08459 812812	www.bankofscotland.co.uk

Mortgage lenders dealing with the self-employed

UCB Homeloans	0845 9401400	www.ucbhomeloans.co.uk
Legal and General	0500 666555	www.landg.co.uk
The Mortgage Business	08457 253253	www.t-m-b-co.uk
Bank of Scotland Centrebank	0645 812812	www.bankofscotland.co.uk

Kensington Mortgage Co.	0800 111020	www.kmc.co.uk
Bank of Ireland	0800 109010	www.boi-mortgages.co.uk
Portman Building Society	01202 292444	www.portman.co.uk

Mortgage brokers

Charcol	0800 718191	www.charcolonline.co.uk
Chase De Vere	020 79307242	www.cdvmortgage.co.uk
Kensington Mortgage Co.	0800 111020	www.kmc.co.uk
Ashley Law	0500 104106	
Highfield Financial Planning	01732 353887	
The Financial Surgery	01794 511099	

Direct mortgage lenders

Bank of Scotland Direct	0800 810810	www.bankofscotland.co.uk
Direct Line	0845 2468100	www.directline.com/mortgages
Egg	0845 6000290	www.egg.com
First Direct	0845 6100103	www.firstdirect.com
Furness Direct	0800 834312	www.furnessbs.co.uk
Leeds and Holbeck Direct	0800 0725726	www.leeds-holbeck.co.uk
Legal and General	08700 100338	www.landg.co.uk
Nationwide Direct	0800 302010	www.nationwide.co.uk
Northern Rock Direct	0845 6050500	www.nrock.co.uk
Standard life Bank	0845 8458450	www.standardlife.com/mortgages

Moneyfacts

Information	*Fax number*
Mortgage Selection	0336 400239*
Commercial Mortgages	0336 400237*
Savings Selection	0336 400238*

Low Cost With Profit Endowment   0336 400850

Full Cost With Profit Endowment   0336 400851

Unit Linked Endowment   0336 400852

Level Term Assurance   0336 400853

*Information lines updated daily.   All other lines updated monthly.

Moneyfacts can be contacted on 01692 500765.

Lenders on the Internet

Abbey National   www.abbeynational.co.uk

Alliance and Leicester   www.alliance-leicester.co.uk/mortgage

Barclays Bank   www.barclays.co.uk

Cheltenham & Gloucester   www.cheltglos.co.uk

Halifax   www.halifax.co.uk

Legal and General   www.legal-and-general.co.uk

Midland Bank   www.midlandbank.co.uk

Nationwide   www.nationwide.co.uk

NatWest   www.natwestgroup.com/nwukhome.html

Other useful websites

Moneynet   www.moneynet.co.uk

Express UK Mortgages   www.ip7.co.uk

Financial Information Net Directory   www.find.co.uk

First Property Search   www.first-mortgage.co.uk

Home Builder (self-build information) www.gold.nct

Homesellers Direct   www.homesellers-direct.co.uk

PropertyNet Buyers Guide   www.god.co.uk

Asserta (mortgages and houses)   www.assertahome.co.uk

Yahoo loan   www.loan.yahoo.com

The Motley Fool (financial advice)   www.fool.co.uk

Virgin money	www.virginmoney.com
Intelligent Finance	www.if.com
FT Your money	www.ftyourmoney.com

Flexible mortgages

Abbey National	0800 555100	www.abbeynational.co.uk
Clydesdale Bank	0800 419000	www.cbonline.co.uk
Egg	08456 000290	www.egg.com
Legal and General Bank	0870 0100338	www.landg.co.uk
Standard Life Bank	0845 8458450	
	www.standardlifebank.com/mortgages	
Virgin Direct*	08456 000001	www.virginone.com
Yorkshire Bank	0800 202122	www.ybonline.co.uk
Yorkshire Building Society	0845 1200100	www.ybs.co.uk
Coventry Building Society	08457 665522	www.covbsoc.co.uk
Hinckley and Rugby Building Society	0800 774499	www.hrbs.co.uk

*Current account mortgage

HOME INSURANCE ON THE INTERNET

Screentrade		www.screentrade.com
Find		www.find.co.uk/insurance
Direct Line	0121 2368877	www.directline.com
Prudential	0800 300300	www.pru.co.uk
Lloyds Bank	0800 834646	www.lloydstsb.com/insurance
Norwich Union	0800 888222	www.norwich-union.co.uk
AA	0800 444777	www.aa.com
Churchill	0800 200 345	www.churchill.com

Abbey National   0800 670660   www.abbeynational.co.uk

ENERGY ADVICE

Save Energy   0345 277200   www.saveenergy.co.uk

Index

BUYING A HOUSE
A step-by-step guide to buying your ideal home

Adam Walker

'With so many pitfalls to avoid when buying a house, it's vital to learn from others. Adam Walker explains how you can move with ease.' *Your New Home.* Management consultant, broadcaster and journalist, Adam Walker has specialised in the residential property market for more than 15 years, training and advising more than 10,000 estate agent staff. He has lectured for the National Association of Estate Agents and the Residential Estate Agency Training and Education Association.

144 pages 1 85703 292 6.

HOW TO MAKE MONEY FROM PROPERTY
The bestselling and expert guide to property investment

Adam Walker

Find out how you can make money from property, with this information-packed guide. It covers how to buy land, commercial property, and holiday homes to let. How to raise finance, deal with tax, agents, developers and builders. Whether you want to become a full-blown property developer, invest in property funds and companies, or simply raise extra cash from renting out spare rooms, this book provides the answers.

128 pages 1 85703 627 1.

MAKING MONEY FROM LETTING
How to buy and let residential property for profit

Moira Stewart

'a comprehensive guide for the new landlord, which treats letting property very much as a business, not just an investment . . . full of good, common sense advice for someone who has never let before.' *Small Landlord's Association.* Includes buying, preparing and managing a property, finding a tenant, letting through agents, understanding taxation, and minimising risk.

160 pages 1 85703 493 7. 2nd edition

MAKING MONEY FROM HOLIDAY LETS
A start-up handbook for buying and letting holiday homes

Jackie Taylor

Whether you live in the country, near the sea, or in a town, this handbook reveals how letting a holiday flat, annexe or cottage can be rewarding and profitable. Discover how to finance and market your business, how and when to use a booking agency, and how to stay on top of paperwork, maintenance – and changeover days! Jackie Taylor left a career as an accountant in London to run a successful holiday cottage business with her husband.

144 pages 1 85703 684 0.

Save £1000s Selling Your Own Home
Learn and estate agent's secrets and make more money selling your home yourself

Tony Booth

With this unique book you benefit from the inside knowledge of an estate agent, cut out the middleman entirely and keep the commission fee in your own pocket. And if you do choose to work with an agent, then by a greater knowledge of the home selling process you'll stay in charge and sell your home faster.

120 pages 1 85703 826 6.

Buy to Let Property Hotspots
Where to buy property and how to let it for profit

Ajay Ahuja & Nick Rampley-Sturgeon

It's still possible to start with very little and make a fortune in property. But increasingly you need to stay ahead of the pack and stick to professional disciplines, techniques and insider tips. And you need to be clear about your aims. This book tells you where and how to buy, and how to rent for maximum gain.

224 pages. 1 85703 888 6.

Starting & Running a B&B
A practival guide to setting up and managing a Bed and Breakfast in the British Isles

Stewart Whyte

More and more people are considering downshifting. Buying a property that can pay for its upkeep and give the owners a comfortable lifestyle is a popular option. Not only has the interest grown in becoming a B&B proprietor, so has the interest by the public in the B&B as a viable short-break option. With this rise in popularity, however, come expectations, and this is where this book comes in. It will tell you all you need to know to make your B&B a truly special place to stay!

256 pages 1 85703 883 5.